Projected Future Climate and Vegetation Changes and Potential Biotic Effects for Fort Benning, Georgia; Fort Hood, Texas; and Fort Irwin, California

By S.L. Shafer, J. Atkins, B.A. Bancroft, P.J. Bartlein, J.J. Lawler, B. Smith, and C.B. Wilsey

Prepared in cooperation with the
U.S. Department of Defense Strategic Environmental Research
and Development Program (SERDP)

Scientific Investigations Report 2011–5099

U.S. Department of the Interior
U.S. Geological Survey

U.S. Department of the Interior
KEN SALAZAR, Secretary

U.S. Geological Survey
Marcia K. McNutt, Director

U.S. Geological Survey, Reston, Virginia: 2012

For more information on the USGS—the Federal source for science about the Earth, its natural and living resources, natural hazards, and the environment, visit http://www.usgs.gov or call 1–888–ASK–USGS.

For an overview of USGS information products, including maps, imagery, and publications, visit http://www.usgs.gov/pubprod

To order this and other USGS information products, visit http://store.usgs.gov

Suggested citation:
Shafer, S.L., Atkins, J., Bancroft, B.A., Bartlein, P.J., Lawler, J.J., Smith, B., and Wilsey, C.B., 2012, Projected climate and vegetation changes and potential biotic effects for Fort Benning, Georgia; Fort Hood, Texas; and Fort Irwin, California: U.S. Geological Survey Scientific Investigations Report 2011–5099, 46 p.

Contents

Abstract 1
Introduction 1
Methods 1
    Study Areas 1
    Climate Data 5
    Bioclimate Data 5
    Projected Vegetation Changes 5
Model Uncertainties and Data Interpretation 6
    Climate Data 6
    Vegetation Models 7
Fort Benning Study Area 8
    Site Description 8
    Disturbance Regimes 8
    Climate 8
    Vegetation 9
        Vegetation Model Parameters 9
        Simulated Historical Vegetation 13
        Simulated Future Vegetation 17
    Implications of Future Climate and Vegetation Changes for Species 18
Fort Hood Study Area 20
    Site Description 20
    Climate 20
    Vegetation 20
        Vegetation Model Parameters 20
        Simulated Historical Vegetation 20
        Simulated Future Vegetation 21
    Implications of Future Climate and Vegetation Changes for Species 24
Fort Irwin Study Area 29
    Site Description 29
    Climate 29
    Vegetation 38
        Vegetation Model Parameters 38
        Simulated Historical Vegetation 38
        Simulated Future Vegetation 38
    Implications of Future Climate and Vegetation Changes for Species 38
Conclusions 39
Acknowledgments 39
References Cited 40

Figures

1–3. Maps displaying:

    1. Elevation (meters) for the Fort Benning study area 2

    2. Elevation (meters) for the Fort Hood study area 3

    3. Elevation (meters) for the Fort Irwin study area...4

    4. Photograph showing a red-cockaded woodpecker (*Picoides borealis*) nest cluster site at Fort Benning, Georgia...9

5–14. Maps displaying:

    5. Mean annual temperature for the Fort Benning study area and the boundary of Fort Benning 11

    6. Mean total annual precipitation for the Fort Benning study area and the boundary of Fort Benning 12

    7. Mean annual growing degree days for the Fort Benning study area and the boundary of Fort Benning 14

    8. Mean annual moisture index for the Fort Benning study area and the boundary of Fort Benning...15

    9. Mean temperature of the coldest month for the Fort Benning study area and the boundary of Fort Benning 16

    10. Mean annual temperature for the Fort Hood study area and the boundary of Fort Hood 22

    11. Mean total annual precipitation for the Fort Hood study area and the boundary of Fort Hood...23

    12. Mean annual growing degree days for the Fort Hood study area and the boundary of Fort Hood 25

    13. Mean annual moisture index for the Fort Hood study area and the boundary of Fort Hood 26

    14. Mean temperature of the coldest month for the Fort Hood study area and the boundary of Fort Hood 27

    15. Photograph showing high quality black-capped vireo *(Vireo atricapilla)* habitat at Fort Hood Military Reservation, Texas 28

    16. Photograph showing open rangeland at Fort Irwin, California...30

17–21. Maps displaying:

    17. Mean annual temperature for the Fort Irwin study area and the boundary of Fort Irwin...32

    18. Mean total annual precipitation for the Fort Irwin study area and the boundary of Fort Irwin...33

    19. Mean annual growing degree days for the Fort Irwin study area and the boundary of Fort Irwin...35

    20. Mean annual moisture index for the Fort Irwin study area and the boundary of Fort Irwin...36

    21. Mean temperature of the coldest month for the Fort Irwin study area and the boundary of Fort Irwin...37

Tables

1. Plant functional types (PFTs) simulated by the models LPJ and LPJ-GUESS for this study 6

2. Mean annual and seasonal temperature and precipitation anomalies for 2070–2099 (30-year mean) for the Fort Benning study area 10

3. Mean annual growing degree days on a 5 degrees Celsius base (GDD5) anomalies, mean annual moisture index, and mean temperature of the coldest month anomalies for 2070–2099 (30-year mean) for the Fort Benning study area 13

4. Mean basal area and density of needleleaved evergreen plant functional type (PFT) individuals greater than 20 years old for 2070–2099 (30-year mean) as simulated by LPJ-GUESS for the Fort Benning study area..17

5. Mean annual and seasonal temperature and precipitation anomalies for 2070–2099 (30-year mean) for the Fort Hood study area...21

6. Mean annual growing degree days on a 5 degrees Celsius base (GDD5) anomalies, mean annual moisture index, and mean temperature of the coldest month anomalies for 2070–2099 (30-year mean) for the Fort Hood study area 24

7. Mean foliar projective cover for needleleaved, broadleaved, and grass plant functional types (PFTs) simulated by LPJ for 1961–1990 (30-year mean) and for 2070–2099 (30-year mean) for the Fort Hood study area 28

8. Mean foliar projective cover of needleleaved evergreen plant functional type (PFT) individuals less than 20 years old for the Fort Hood study area (2070–2099 30-year mean) as simulated by LPJ-GUESS with fires suppressed ("no fire") and with fires simulated ("fire")............................29

9. Mean annual and seasonal temperature and precipitation anomalies for 2070–2099 (30-year mean) for the Fort Irwin study area 31

10. Mean annual growing degree days on a 5 degrees Celsius base (GDD5) anomalies, mean annual moisture index, and mean temperature of the coldest month anomalies for 2070–2099 (30-year mean) for the Fort Irwin study area 34

11. Mean annual grass cover anomalies and fire return intervals for 2070–2099 (30-year mean) as simulated by LPJ for the Fort Irwin study area.................................39

Conversion Factors

SI to Inch/Pound

Multiply	By	To obtain
Length		
centimeter (cm)	0.3937	inch (in.)
millimeter (mm)	0.03937	inch (in.)
meter (m)	3.281	foot (ft)
kilometer (km)	0.6214	mile (mi)
Area		
hectare (ha)	2.471	acre
square kilometer (km^2)	247.1	acre
square meter (m^2)	10.76	square foot (ft^2)
hectare (ha)	0.003861	square mile (mi^2)
square kilometer (km^2)	0.3861	square mile (mi^2)

Temperature in degrees Celsius (°C) may be converted to degrees Fahrenheit (°F) as follows:

°F=(1.8×°C)+32

Vertical coordinate information is referenced to the North American Vertical Datum of 1988 (NAVD 88)

Horizontal coordinate information is referenced to the North American Datum of 1983 (NAD 83)

Altitude, as used in this report, refers to distance above the vertical datum.

Abbreviations

AET	Actual evapotranspiration
AOGCM	Atmosphere-ocean general circulation model
CMIP3	Coupled Model Intercomparison Project, phase 3
CO_2	Carbon dioxide
CRU	Climatic Research Unit
FACE	Free-air CO_2 enrichment
FPC	Foliar projective cover
GDD5	Growing degree days calculated on a 5 degrees Celsius base
ISAM	Integrated Science Assessment Model
IPCC	Intergovernmental Panel on Climate Change
PCMDI	Program for Climate Model Diagnosis and Intercomparison
PDSI	Palmer Drought Severity Index
PET	Potential evapotranspiration
PFT	Plant functional type
PPM	Parts per million
UTM	Universal Transverse Mercator
WCRP	World Climate Research Programme

Projected Future Climate and Vegetation Changes and Potential Biotic Effects for Fort Benning, Georgia; Fort Hood, Texas; and Fort Irwin, California

By S.L. Shafer,[1] J. Atkins,[2,5] B.A. Bancroft,[2,6] P.J. Bartlein,[3] J.J. Lawler,[2] B. Smith,[4] and C.B. Wilsey[2]

Abstract

The responses of species and ecosystems to future climate changes will present challenges for conservation and natural resource managers attempting to maintain both species populations and essential habitat. This report describes projected future changes in climate and vegetation for three study areas surrounding the military installations of Fort Benning, Georgia, Fort Hood, Texas, and Fort Irwin, California. We describe projected climate changes for the time period 2070–2099 (30-year mean) as compared to 1961–1990 (30-year mean) for each study area using data simulated by the coupled atmosphere-ocean general circulation models CCSM3, CGCM3.1(T47), and UKMO-HadCM3, run under the B1, A1B, and A2 future greenhouse gas emissions scenarios. We use these climate data to simulate potential changes in important components of the vegetation for each study area using LPJ, a dynamic global vegetation model, and LPJ-GUESS, a dynamic vegetation model optimized for regional studies. The simulated vegetation results are compared with observed vegetation data for the study areas. We discuss the potential effects of the simulated future climate and vegetation changes for species and habitats of management concern in each study area, with a particular focus on federally listed threatened and endangered species.

Introduction

Climate is projected to change over the coming decades in ways that will affect many species and ecosystems in the United States (Karl and others, 2009). Temperatures are projected to increase, precipitation may become more variable in some regions, and the frequency and intensity of extreme climate events, such as hurricanes, may change (Meehl and others, 2007b; Karl and others, 2009). These and other projected climate changes will affect species and ecosystems in many different ways, including altering species distributions, driving phenological changes, and affecting disturbance regimes (Parmesan, 2006; Parry and others, 2007). Projected climate changes will occur in areas that already have experienced significant land use effects over the past centuries, increasing the challenges for land managers attempting to maintain species and ecosystems of conservation concern.

This report summarizes projected climate and vegetation simulations for three study areas that encompass the military installations of Fort Benning, Georgia, Fort Hood, Texas, and Fort Irwin, California (figs.1–3). The experimental protocols and data described in this report were designed specifically to provide climate and vegetation data for modeling the potential effects of climate change on three species of management concern, the red-cockaded woodpecker (*Picoides borealis*) in the Fort Benning study area, the black-capped vireo (*Vireo atricapilla*) in the Fort Hood study area, and the desert tortoise (*Gopherus agassizii*) in the Fort Irwin study area. We use these data to describe some of the potential effects of future climate and vegetation changes for these and other species of management concern within each of the study areas.

Methods

Study Areas

Grids in Universal Transverse Mercator (UTM) projections were developed for each study area using 1,000-meter (m) grids for the Fort Benning and Fort Irwin study areas (figs. 1 and 3). A 960-m grid was used for the Fort Hood study area (fig. 2) to match the spatial resolution of datasets being used to model the potential effects of climate change on the black-capped vireo as part of a U.S. Department of Defense

---

[1]U.S. Geological Survey, Corvallis, Oregon.

[2]School of Forest Resources, University of Washington, Seattle, Washington.

[3]Department of Geography, University of Oregon, Eugene, Oregon.

[4]Department of Earth and Ecosystem Sciences, Lund University, Lund, Sweden.

[5]Current address: Scientific Certification Systems, Emeryville, California.

[6]Current address: Department of Biology, Southern Utah University, Cedar City, Utah.

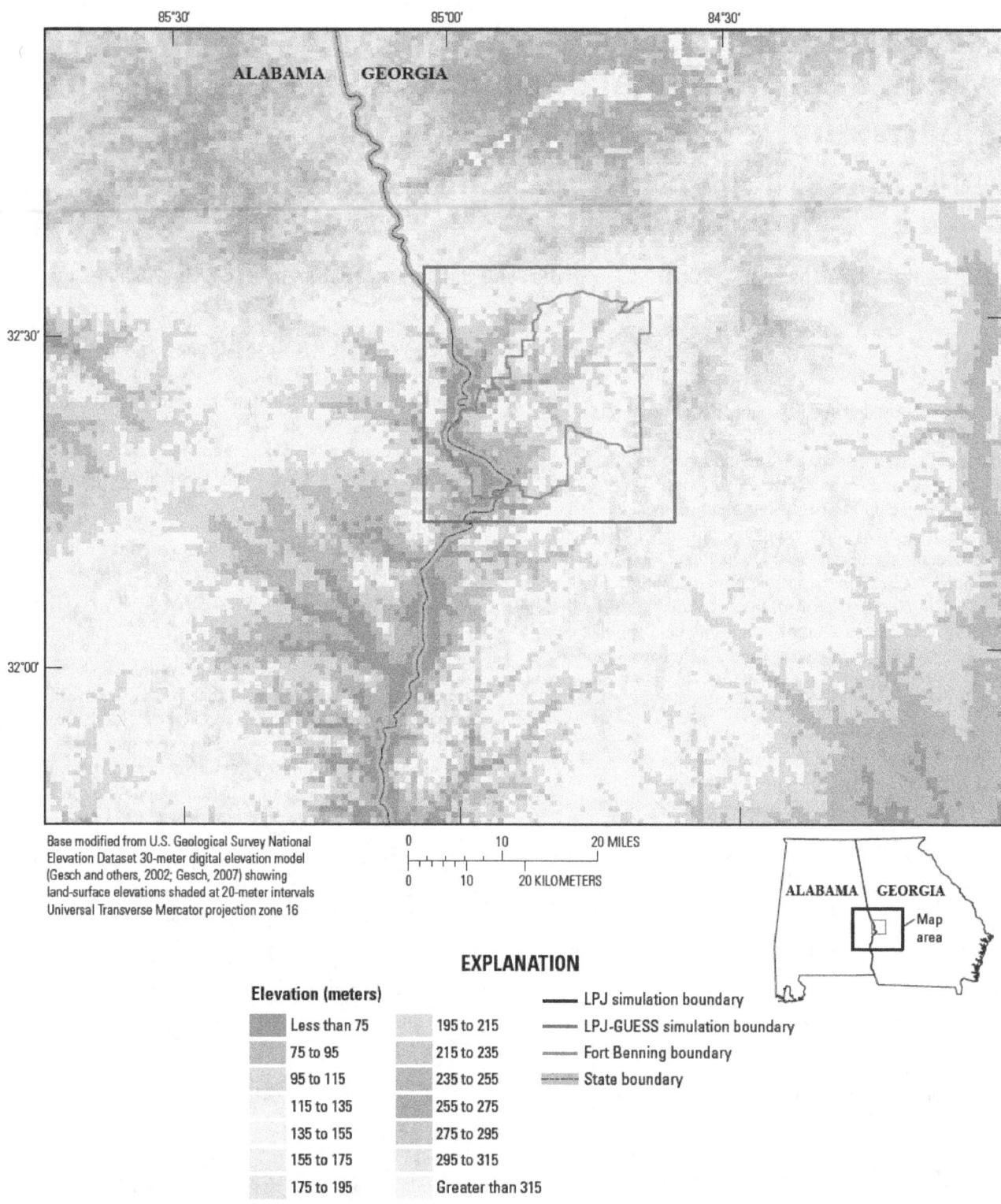

Figure 1. Elevation (meters) for the Fort Benning study area.

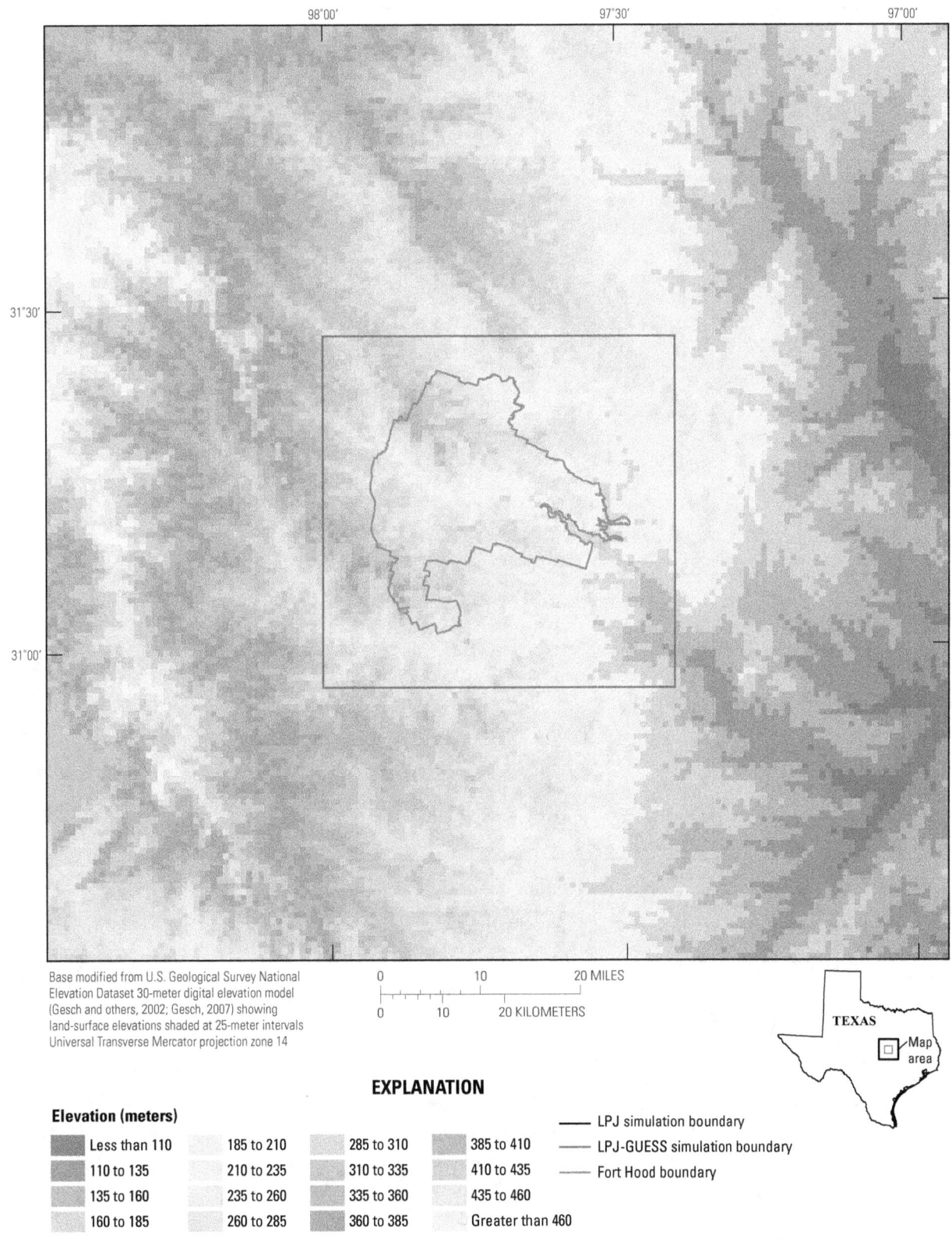

Base modified from U.S. Geological Survey National
Elevation Dataset 30-meter digital elevation model
(Gesch and others, 2002; Gesch, 2007) showing
land-surface elevations shaded at 25-meter intervals
Universal Transverse Mercator projection zone 14

EXPLANATION

Elevation (meters)

Less than 110	185 to 210	285 to 310	385 to 410
110 to 135	210 to 235	310 to 335	410 to 435
135 to 160	235 to 260	335 to 360	435 to 460
160 to 185	260 to 285	360 to 385	Greater than 460

—— LPJ simulation boundary

—— LPJ-GUESS simulation boundary

—— Fort Hood boundary

Figure 2.   Elevation (meters) for the Fort Hood study area.

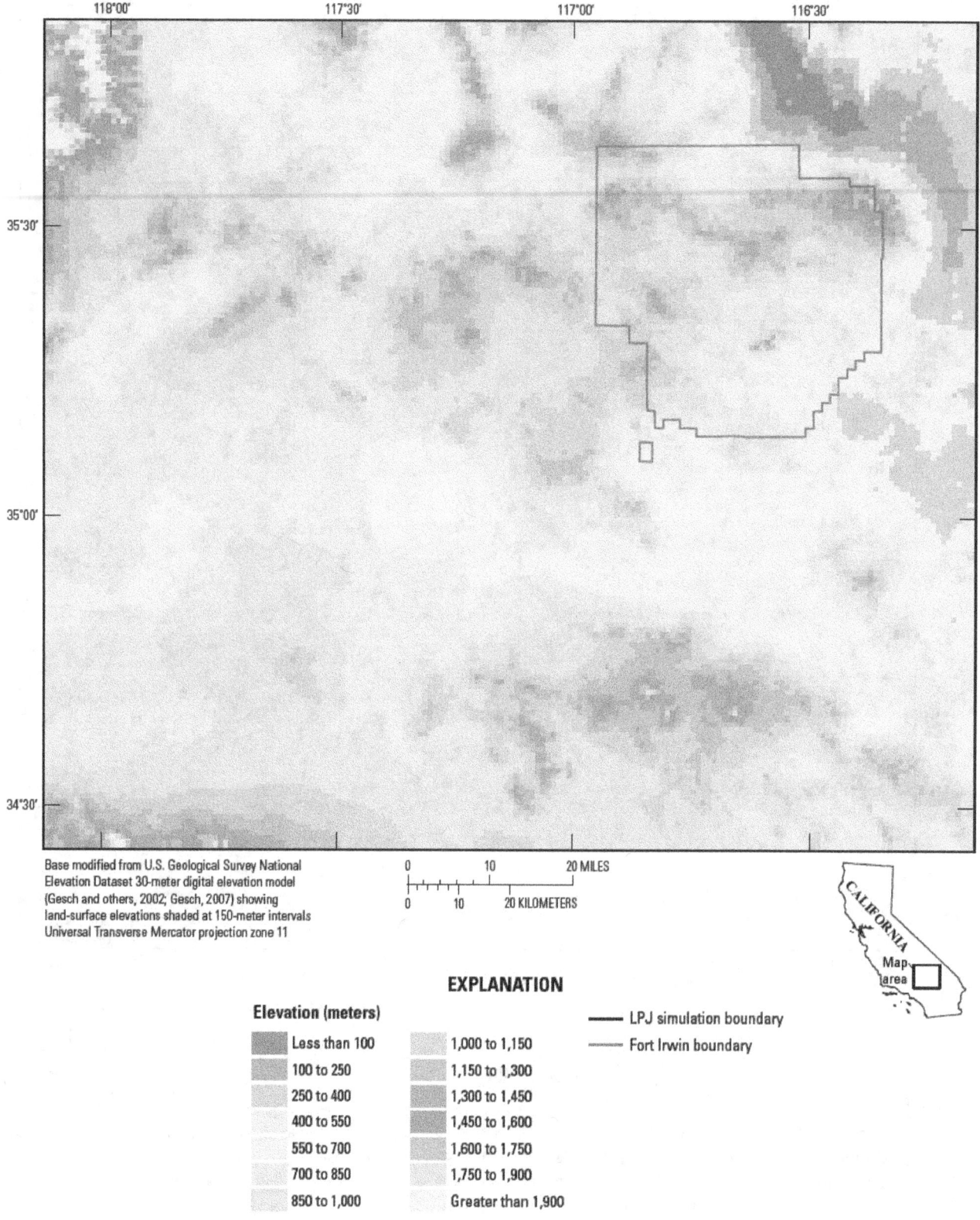

Figure 3.   Elevation (meters) for the Fort Irwin study area.

Strategic Environmental Research and Development Program (SERDP)-funded study (SI-1541). For each study area grid point, we assigned the elevation value from the 1-arc-second National Elevation Dataset (Gesch and others, 2002; Gesch, 2007) grid cell within which each study area grid point was located. In the following text, references to each study area refer to the entire area displayed in figures 1–3.

Climate Data

Historical long-term mean climate data from the University of East Anglia's Climatic Research Unit (CRU) CL 1.0 and CL 2.0 1961–1990 (30-year mean) global datasets (New and others, 1999; New and others, 2002) were downscaled to each study area grid point using a moving window or local regression method to estimate the lapse rates of each variable. These local lapse rates were used to make elevationally adjusted interpolations of the CRU long-term mean climate data onto the analysis grid. Downscaled variables included monthly mean temperature, in degrees Celsius (°C); total precipitation, in millimeters (mm); and mean sunshine (percent) from the CRU CL 2.0 dataset and monthly mean cloud cover (percent) from the CRU CL 1.0 dataset. To produce monthly time series data for the 20th-century, monthly anomalies for temperature, precipitation, and sunshine (estimated from cloud cover data) were calculated for each month in the 1901–2002 CRU TS 2.1 global 30-minute gridded dataset (Mitchell and Jones, 2005) using a 1961–1990 30-year mean base period. Temperature anomalies were calculated as differences (each monthly value minus the 1961–1990 30-year mean base period value) and precipitation and sunshine anomalies were calculated as ratios (each monthly value divided by the 1961–1990 30-year mean base period value). These anomalies were interpolated to each study area grid point using a geographic-distance-weighted bilinear interpolation method and then applied to the downscaled CRU CL 2.0 1961–1990 30-year mean value for each climate variable at each grid point to create monthly time series data for those points.

Future climate data for each study area were created by downscaling projected climate simulations from three coupled atmosphere-ocean general circulation models (AOGCMs), CCSM3 (Collins and others, 2006a), CGCM3.1(T47) (Scinocca and others, 2008), and UKMO-HadCM3 (Pope and others, 2000). Each AOGCM was run under the B1, A1B, and A2 greenhouse gas emissions scenarios (Nakicenovic and others, 2000) as part of the World Climate Research Programme's (WCRP) Coupled Model Intercomparison Project, phase 3 (CMIP3) (Meehl and others, 2007a). The AOGCM data were obtained from the CMIP3 multimodel dataset archived by the Program for Climate Model Diagnosis and Intercomparison (PCMDI; *http://www-pcmdi.llnl.gov/ipcc/about_ipcc.php*).

For each AOGCM simulation, anomalies of monthly mean temperature, total precipitation, and cloud cover for the years 2001–2099 were calculated against a 1961–1990 30-year mean base period from the corresponding AOGCM 20th-century simulation (see *http://www-pcmdi.llnl.gov/ipcc/time_correspondence_summary.htm*). Temperature anomalies were calculated as differences (monthly value minus 1961–1990 30-year mean base period value) and precipitation and cloud cover anomalies were calculated as ratios (monthly value divided by 1961–1990 30-year mean base period value). The future climate anomalies were downscaled to each study area grid point using geographic-distance-weighted bilinear interpolation. The interpolated anomalies for each month from 2001–2099 were applied to the interpolated 1961–1990 30-year monthly mean data for each grid point to create downscaled monthly future temperature, precipitation, and sunshine (calculated from cloud cover) data.

Bioclimate Data

Bioclimate variables (for example, growing degree days) are climate-derived variables that represent important physiological limits for many species (for example, lethal minimum temperatures) or are considered proxies for important environmental controls on the distributions of both plant and animal taxa. Bioclimate variables were calculated for each study area from the modern and simulated future climate data for the period 1901–2099 using an approach modified from Cramer and Prentice (1988) and soil data from the CONUS-SOIL dataset (Miller and White, 1998). We evaluated growing degree days (5 °C base), mean temperature of the coldest month (°C), and a moisture index calculated as annual actual evapotranspiration (AET) for a generic vegetation type divided by annual potential evapotranspiration (PET; Prentice and others, 1992).

Projected Vegetation Changes

We simulated vegetation for each study area using two different models. LPJ (Lund-Potsdam-Jena, version January 2004), a dynamic global vegetation model (Sitch and others, 2003), was used to simulate dominant vegetation changes for each study area (figs. 1–3). LPJ-GUESS (version 030124, Smith and others, 2001), a dynamic vegetation model optimized for regional studies, was used to simulate vegetation changes for a smaller domain surrounding Fort Benning and Fort Hood (delineated by the gray boxes in figures 1 and 2). Both LPJ and LPJ-GUESS simulate vegetation in the form of plant functional types (PFTs), such as needleleaved evergreen PFTs (table 1). These PFTs can be combined to represent major biomes and habitat types (for example, forest and grassland). The models are run at a monthly time-step to simulate the transient responses of vegetation to climate change. Both models also simulate the physiological response of vegetation to increased atmospheric carbon dioxide (CO_2) concentrations, which is an important process for projecting vegetation responses to climate change (Hickler and others, 2008).

Table 1.   Plant functional types (PFTs) simulated by the models LPJ (Sitch and others, 2003) and LPJ-GUESS (Smith and others, 2001) for this study. All non-grass PFTs are considered woody.

Plant functional types	
LPJ	**LPJ-GUESS**
Tropical broadleaved evergreen	Temperate needleleaved evergreen, shade tolerant
Tropical broadleaved raingreen	Temperate needleleaved evergreen, shade intolerant
Temperate needleleaved evergreen	Temperate broadleaved summergreen, shade tolerant
Temperate broadleaved evergreen	Temperate broadleaved summergreen, shade intolerant
Temperate broadleaved summergreen	Temperate broadleaved evergreen
Boreal needleleaved evergreen	Grass (C3)
Boreal needleleaved summergreen	
Boreal broadleaved summergreen	
Grass (C3)	
Grass (C4)	

LPJ and LPJ-GUESS were run using the interpolated monthly temperature, precipitation, and sunshine data. A spin-up period of 800 years was used to simulate vegetation from bare ground and to allow carbon pools to equilibrate for each study area grid point. Climate data for the spin-up period consisted of repeated 1901–1930 monthly temperature, precipitation, and sunshine data. The temperature data used for the spin-up period were detrended by using locally weighted regression (Cleveland, 1993) to estimate the long-term trend in the temperature data for each grid cell and then subtracting the long-term trend values from the data in order to remove any such trend. Following the spin-up period, each vegetation model was run for an additional 199 years using the monthly climate data downscaled from the CRU CL 2.0 and CRU TS 2.1 datasets for the years 1901–2000 and the downscaled future climate data for the years 2001–2099. We used 20th-century historical and projected future global mean annual atmospheric CO_2 concentrations from the Integrated Science Assessment Model (ISAM) reference case simulations (Prentice and others 2001), which produced mean annual atmospheric CO_2 values of 549 parts per million (ppm) for the B1 scenario, 717 ppm for the A1B scenario, and 856 ppm for the A2 scenario by the year 2100.

The vegetation models, although similar in some ways, are different in their specific assumptions and performance. LPJ is an area-based model that simulates an average individual PFT for each grid cell; individual differences in age, size, and resource use are not distinguished. LPJ-GUESS simulates the average individual for each cohort (age class) of a PFT in each of a number of replicate patches, in which PFTs and individuals compete for light and soil resources. LPJ-GUESS was used to evaluate simulated changes in the size and age of PFT average individuals through time. The PFT parameters of both models were adjusted to better represent

the nonstressed maximum age and relative fire resistance of the major plant taxa at each site. In many cases detailed physiological and life history data were not available for key plant species. In these cases, we used data for related species or species with similar physiological characteristics.

Model Uncertainties and Data Interpretation

The potential future climate and vegetation data used in this study include a number of uncertainties that affect the ways in which these data can be interpreted and used. These uncertainties range from assumptions about social and political decisions that will affect the rate and magnitude of future climate changes to limitations in our understanding of the physical processes that control the behavior of the climate system. Below we describe some of the uncertainties associated with each type of data.

Climate Data

The historical climate data used in this study were derived from the CRU CL 1.0 (New and others 1999), CRU CL 2.0 (New and others, 2002), and CRU TS 2.1 (Mitchell and Jones, 2005) gridded global climate datasets. These datasets use observed climate data from existing and historical climate station records to estimate climate data for locations for which climate records do not exist. The quantity and quality of the observed climate data used in developing the CRU CL 1.0, CRU CL 2.0 and CRU TS 2.1 datasets varies both spatially and temporally. Some of the limitations of these data are described in New and others (1999, 2000) and Mitchell and Jones (2005). To create gridded climate data across our study areas, we further interpolated these gridded climate data to each grid point in the study area. Thus, the gridded climate data used in this study are not direct climate measurements at each study area grid point but are estimates of climate based on observed data. Daly (2006) and Daly and others (2008) describe some of the assumptions and limitations with these types of gridded climate data.

The future climate simulations described in this study are numerical model projections of future climates. In general, there is relatively more agreement among AOGCM simulations of future temperature changes than among AOGCM simulations of future precipitation changes (Dai, 2006). The current generation of AOGCMs tend to overestimate the frequency of small volume precipitation events and underestimate the frequency of large volume precipitation events (Randall and others, 2007), making it difficult to estimate how future temperature and precipitation changes will interact to affect species and habitat. Some of the uncertainties in climate projections are the result of limitations in the ability of AOGCMs to accurately simulate complex climate processes, such as cloud dynamics (Randall and others, 2007). Other uncertainties are inherent in the climate system and involve nonlinear and stochastic processes that are not modeled adequately with deterministic models, such as the initiation of cumulus convection (Giorgi, 2005). Giorgi (2005), Giorgi and Diffenbaugh (2008), and Bader and others (2008) provide a discussion of some of the uncertainties associated with future climate simulations.

In this study we used data from three AOGCMs that were each run using three different greenhouse gas emissions scenarios (B1, A1B, and A2). The scenarios, described in Nakicenovic and others (2000), incorporate information about the future rate and magnitude of various greenhouse gas emissions based on assumptions about potential future economic, political, and social decisions in combination with technological advances that may occur in the future. The B1 scenario assumes increasing development and use of energy-efficient technologies with global population increasing until the middle of the 21st-century and then declining. The A1B scenario assumes rapid future economic growth and technological change accompanied by increases in global population until the middle of the 21st-century followed by decreases in population. The A2 scenario assumes that global population continues to increase in the 21st-century with less rapid technological change than the other two scenarios. There are many other potential future greenhouse gas emissions scenarios that are possible and thus the projected future climate data used in this study represent only part of the range of potential future changes that are projected by different combinations of AOGCMs and emissions scenarios (Meehl and others, 2007b).

The AOGCMs simulate climate at relatively coarse spatial scales, with a single AOGCM grid cell often covering thousands of square kilometers (km^2). We downscaled the AOGCM simulations to our study area grid points by calculating, interpolating, and applying anomalies, a process sometimes referred to as the delta-change method of downscaling (Hay and others, 2000; Mote and Salathé, 2010). This simple downscaling method allows many AOGCM simulations to be downscaled relatively quickly, but the method includes a number of assumptions and limitations. For example, this downscaling method does not incorporate many of the physical processes that can affect climate at finer spatial scales, such as rain shadows or cold air drainage produced by topography. There are many other methods for downscaling AOGCM simulations to finer spatial resolutions, and different methods would produce different patterns of climate change across the study areas. Maraun and others (2010) and Wiens and Bachelet (2010) discuss some of the uncertainties associated with downscaled climate data and their use.

Vegetation Models

The vegetation models used in this study are mechanistic models that simulate some, but not all, of the physical and biological processes affecting the character and distribution of vegetation (Smith and others, 2001; Sitch and others, 2003). Some of the processes simulated by the models are not well understood, in general or in terms of the differential responses of different PFTs. In such cases, the processes are represented in a manner that reflects the current state of empirical and theoretical understanding. An example is the simulated carbon assimilation and growth responses of plants to changes in atmospheric CO_2 concentrations, for which physiological studies and free-air CO_2 enrichment (FACE) experiments generally indicate a positive response, although negative biogeochemical feedbacks might reduce this response on longer time scales (Hickler and others, 2008). Additionally, a number of processes in LPJ-GUESS are stochastic, such as the simulation of mortality in the PFT "population" (Smith and others, 2001). Zaehle and others (2005) and Wramneby and others (2008) discuss implications of the parameter-based uncertainties in LPJ and LPJ-GUESS on the simulated carbon balance and dynamics of vegetation.

We used the vegetation simulations in this study to evaluate potential future changes in vegetation across each study area. The simulations provide insight into aspects of the potential changes in PFT distributions, community structure and succession in response to future climate shifts, but also have limitations in both their spatial and temporal accuracy that affect how the model results can be interpreted. For example, the vegetation simulations resolve elevational variations in vegetation associated with climate gradients but they do not consider the effects on vegetation of many other local variables, such as aspect and slope, that can significantly affect the temperature and soil moisture of a site and thus finer scale spatial patterns of vegetation. Different species with similar structural and functional characteristics (that is, belonging to the same PFT) were not distinguished; individual tree species can be distinguished in LPJ-GUESS (Hickler and others, 2004; Koca and others, 2006), but this is not possible in the more generalized framework of LPJ. The models simulate the effects on vegetation of fire occurrence, but the spatial and temporal patterns of actual fire occurrence can be affected by both natural processes (for example, lightning) and human activities (Bartlein and others, 2008) that are not represented in the models. In addition, the vegetation patterns observed across the three study areas have been affected by many factors, including past land uses (for example, logging) and disturbance events (for example, fire and fire suppression) for which detailed historical records do not exist. These historical factors are not explicitly incorporated into the vegetation model simulations, which affects not only the simulated vegetation accuracy for particular locations but also the accuracy at various points in time throughout the simulations.

Fort Benning Study Area

Site Description

The Fort Benning study area (21,976 km²) spans the border between central Alabama and central Georgia in the southeastern United States (fig. 1). It is centered on Fort Benning and lies near the Coastal Plain-Piedmont Fall Line, which represents the geologic transition from the Appalachian Highlands to the southeastern coastal plain of the United States (Olsen and others, 2007). The area generally is hilly with estimated elevations of the study area grid points ranging from approximately 51 m to approximately 405 m above sea level (Gesch and others, 2002).

The Fort Benning study area is in the coniferous-broadleaved semievergreen forest ecoregion defined by Bailey (1997). Oak-hickory-pine forest is the dominant potential natural vegetation for the region (Küchler, 1993). A field study by Dilustro and others (2002) concluded that undisturbed upland sites within the boundaries of Fort Benning consisted of pine-oak-hickory forest, ranging from sandhills scrub oak-pine to pine-hardwood or oak-hickory dominated forest. This description of the undisturbed vegetation agrees well with Küchler's (1993) potential natural vegetation classification of oak-hickory-pine forest for the region. Tree species found across the study area include pines, such as longleaf pine (*Pinus palustris*), shortleaf pine (*P. echinata*) and loblolly pine (*P. taeda*), various species of oak, such as southern red oak (*Quercus falcata*), white oak (*Q. alba*), and water oak (*Q. nigra*), and other broadleaf species, such as shagbark hickory (*Carya ovata*) and tulip tree (*Liriodendron tulipifera*) (fig. 4; Dilustro and others, 2002). The region has numerous sand exposures and sandy ridge tops that support more xeric vegetation communities, including longleaf pine forests and woodlands (Christensen, 2000; Collins and others, 2006b). A number of studies have described various aspects of the vegetation within the boundaries of Fort Benning, including Dale and others (2002), Dilustro and others (2002), and Collins and others (2006b).

Disturbance Regimes

Fire plays an important role in the maintenance of longleaf pine forests in the southeastern United States (Heyward, 1939; Van Lear and others, 2005). Prior to Euro-American settlement, pine forests dominated large areas of the region (Varner and Kush, 2004). These open forests were maintained by relatively frequent fires, both the result of naturally occurring wildfires as well as fires that may have been started by Native Americans in the region. Fire history records from longleaf pine stands indicate a mean fire return interval of approximately 3 years prior to Euro-American settlement of the region (Bale, 2009). Bale (2009) found that fire frequency in longleaf pine stands in northeast Alabama increased slightly during Euro-American settlement before decreasing in the early 1900s with the initiation of more active fire suppression activities. Dilustro and others (2002) note that, of the 32 upland forest sites they examined at Fort Benning, the proportion of pine in the canopy increased with increasing disturbance from land-use activities, including military activities and fire. In the absence of disturbance, pine-oak forests became increasingly dominated by shade-tolerant species, such as some oak species in the region (Gilliam and Platt, 1999).

In addition to changes in fire frequency, the Fort Benning study area has undergone significant land-use changes during the past few centuries (Dale and others, 2002; Dilustro and others, 2006). Euro-American settlers cleared land for agriculture and large areas of the region have been logged at various times in the past (Van Lear and others, 2005). Fort Benning was farmed until 1945 when all private landowners were removed (Dale and others, 2002). More recently, military activities at Fort Benning have produced disturbances of various intensities (Maloney and others, 2008). Land-management activities, such as prescribed burns, also have contributed to vegetation disturbance at the site (Maloney and others, 2008).

Climate

The estimated 1961–1990 30-year mean temperatures for the Fort Benning study area are 17.7 °C annually, 17.7 °C in spring (March–May), 26.3 °C in summer (June–August), 18.4 °C in fall (September–November) and 8.4 °C in winter (December–February). The estimated 1961–1990 30-year mean precipitation for the study area is 1,276 mm annually, 348 mm in spring (March–May), 336 mm in summer (June–August), 228 mm in fall (September–November) and 364 mm in winter (December–February). The 1961–1990 30-year mean bioclimatic values are 4,663 GDD5, 0.8154 for the moisture index (AET/PET), and 6.41 °C for the mean temperature of the coldest month.

Projected future mean annual temperature changes for the study area for 2070–2099 (30-year mean) range from an increase of 1.58 °C simulated by CCSM3 under the B1 emissions scenario to 4.66 °C simulated by UKMO-HadCM3

Figure 4. A red-cockaded woodpecker (*Picoides borealis*) nest cluster site at Fort Benning, Georgia. Nest trees are marked with white stripes. This site is typical of good red-cockaded woodpecker habitat with mature pine trees and an open understory (Photograph taken by J.J. Lawler, 2007).

under the A2 emissions scenario (table 2, fig. 5). Projected future mean annual precipitation changes for the study area for 2070–2099 (30-year mean) range from a 1 percent increase simulated by CGCM3.1(T47) under the B1 emissions scenario to a 23 percent increase simulated by UKMO-HadCM3 under the A1B emissions scenario (table 2, fig. 6).

Both GDD5 and moisture index (AET/PET) values are projected to increase under all nine AOGCM and emissions scenario combinations (table 3, figs. 7 and 8). The moisture index values increase from 0.8154 (1961–1990 30-year mean) to values ranging from 0.8232 to 0.9355 (2070–2099 30-year mean) under the projected future climates (table 3). Mean temperature of the coldest month also increases under all nine AOGCM and emissions scenario combinations (table 3, fig. 9) with increases ranging from 1.52 °C simulated by CCSM3 under the B1 emissions scenario to 3.38 °C simulated by UKMO-HadCM3 under the A1B emissions scenario (2070–2099 30-year mean).

Vegetation

LPJ was used to simulate biome changes for the Fort Benning study area. LPJ-GUESS was used to simulate

changes in basal area and mean age of the needleleaved evergreen PFT for the smaller area surrounding Fort Benning (fig. 1). These two variables represent characteristics of longleaf pine forests that provide important habitat for the red-cockaded woodpecker (*Picoides borealis*), a species of management concern in the region.

Vegetation Model Parameters

For LPJ we used the model parameters described in tables 1 and 2 of Sitch and others (2003) except for fire resistance values. Fire resistance in LPJ for the evergreen needleleaved PFT was set to 0.50 to represent the increased fire resistance of longleaf pines. This value was based on observed adult longleaf pine mortality from prescribed fires reported by Varner and others (2007). The fire resistance parameters for the other woody PFTs were set to 0.12. In LPJ-GUESS the fire resistance parameter for the needleleaved evergreen PFT was also set to 0.50. The fire resistance parameter for the shade-tolerant broadleaved summergreen PFT was set at 0.12 to represent the increased mortality following fires of species such as laurel oak (*Q. hemisphaerica*) (Varner and others, 2005; Collins and others 2006b). The fire resistance parameter

Table 2. Mean annual and seasonal temperature (degrees Celsius) and precipitation (percent) anomalies for 2070–2099 (30-year mean) for the Fort Benning study area. Anomalies were calculated from downscaled CCSM3 (Collins and others, 2006a), CGCM3.1(T47) (Scinocca and others, 2008), and UKMO-HadCM3 (Pope and others, 2000) coupled atmosphere-ocean general circulation model simulations produced using the B1, A1B, and A2 greenhouse gas emissions scenarios.

Model simulation	Greenhouse gas emissions scenario					
	B1		A1B		A2	
	Temperature[1] (degrees Celsius)	Precipitation[2] (percent)	Temperature[1] (degrees Celsius)	Precipitation[2] (percent)	Temperature[1] (degrees Celsius)	Precipitation[2] (percent)
Annual						
CCSM3	+1.58	+13	+2.92	+7	+3.80	+10
CGCM3.1(T47)	+2.06	+1	+2.78	+5	+3.62	+7
UKMO-HadCM3	+3.19	+13	+4.28	+23	+4.66	+4
December–February						
CCSM3	+1.49	+11	+2.61	-5	+3.34	-8
CGCM3.1(T47)	+1.40	+3	+2.04	+14	+2.49	+4
UKMO-HadCM3	+3.37	+9	+3.94	+15	+3.12	+8
March–May						
CCSM3	+1.94	+9	+3.26	+8	+4.05	+15
CGCM3.1(T47)	+1.54	+1	+2.77	+1	+3.66	+3
UKMO-HadCM3	+2.94	+19	+4.39	+27	+4.33	+2
June–August						
CCSM3	+1.35	+25	+2.56	+24	+3.70	+23
CGCM3.1(T47)	+2.56	-6	+3.22	+3	+4.21	+6
UKMO-HadCM3	+3.31	+6	+4.80	+19	+6.32	-6
September–November						
CCSM3	+1.54	+7	+3.27	+2	+4.10	+10
CGCM3.1(T47)	+2.75	+6	+3.09	+3	+4.14	+15
UKMO-HadCM3	+3.13	+16	+3.98	+31	+4.85	+13

[1]Temperature anomalies were calculated as 2070–2099 (30-year mean) simulated temperature minus 1961–1990 (30-year mean) simulated temperature.

[2]Precipitation anomalies were calculated by multiplying by 100 the quotient of 2070–2099 (30-year mean) simulated precipitation divided by 1961–1990 (30-year mean) simulated precipitation.

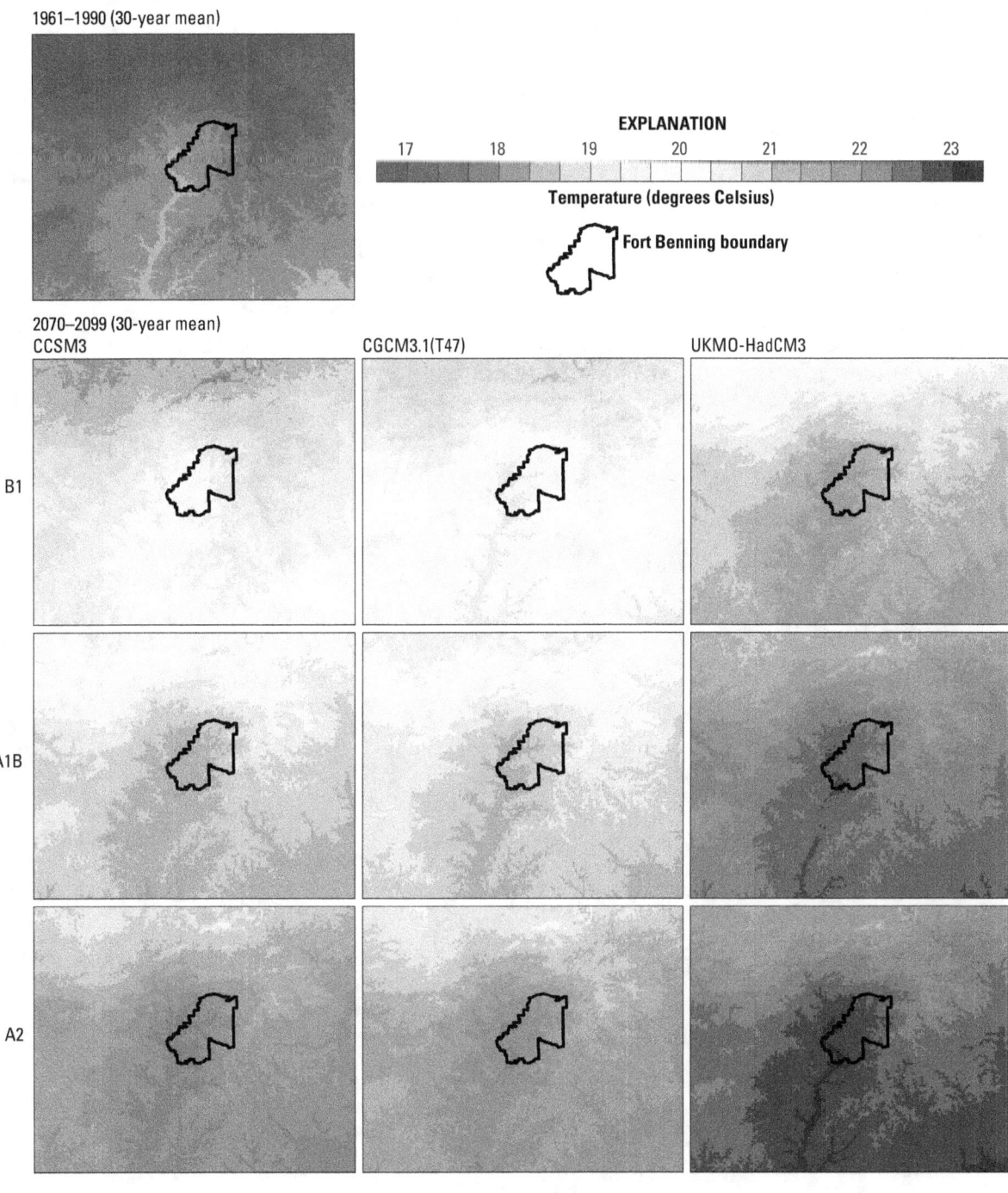

Figure 5. Mean annual temperature (degrees Celsius) for the Fort Benning study area and the boundary of Fort Benning (black line). Top row: 1961–1990 (30-year mean) mean annual temperature calculated from downscaled CRU CL 2.0 (New and others, 2002) and CRU TS 2.1 (Mitchell and Jones, 2005) data. Bottom rows: 2070–2099 (30-year mean) mean annual temperature calculated from downscaled CCSM3 (Collins and others, 2006a), CGCM3.1(T47) (Scinocca and others, 2008), and UKMO-HadCM3 (Pope and others, 2000) simulations produced using the B1, A1B, and A2 greenhouse gas emissions scenarios.

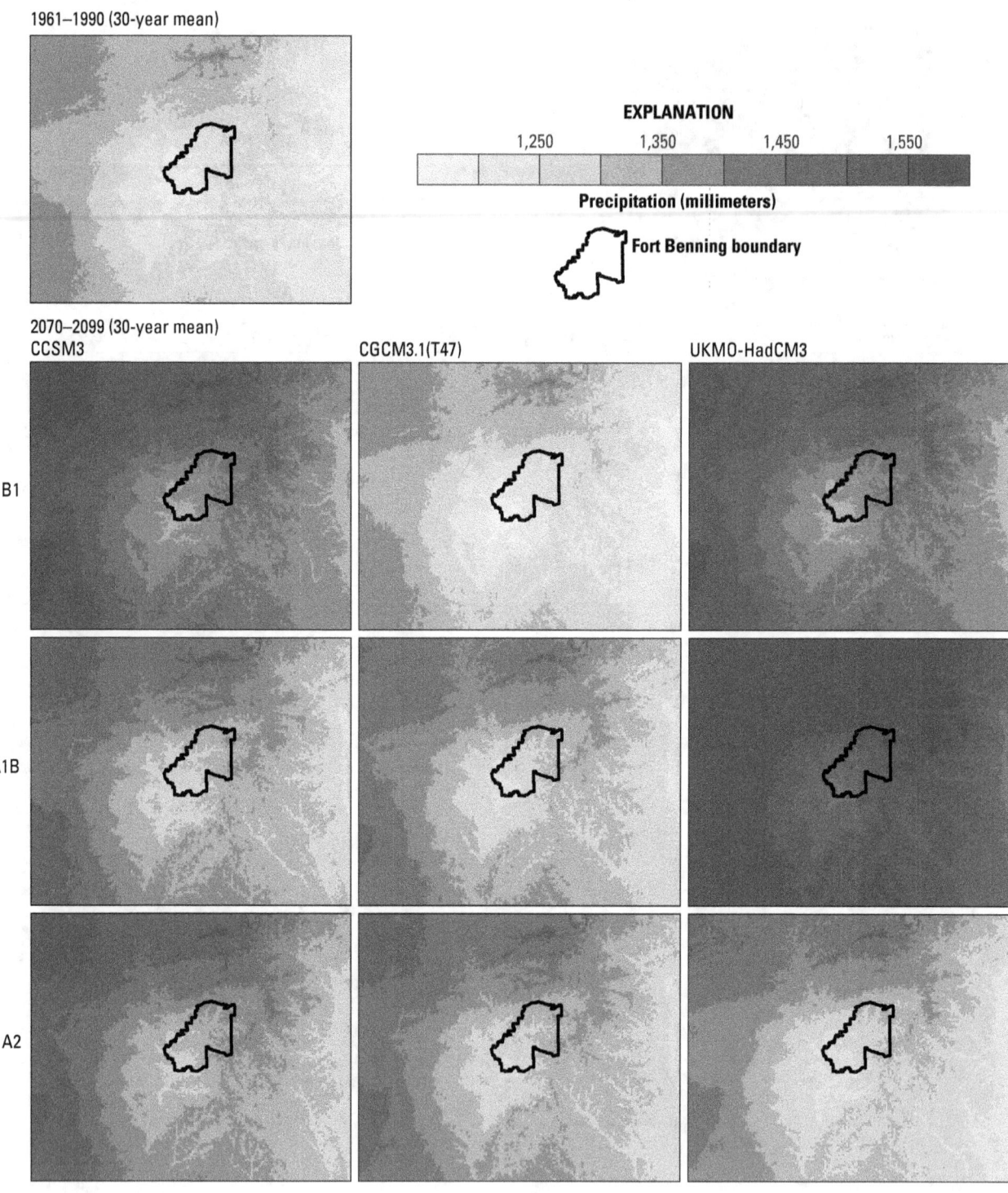

Figure 6.   Mean total annual precipitation (millimeters) for the Fort Benning study area and the boundary of Fort Benning (black line). Top row: 1961–1990 (30-year mean) mean total annual precipitation calculated from downscaled CRU CL 2.0 (New and others, 2002) and CRU TS 2.1 (Mitchell and Jones, 2005) data. Bottom rows: 2070–2099 (30-year mean) mean total annual precipitation calculated from downscaled CCSM3 (Collins and others, 2006a), CGCM3.1(T47) (Scinocca and others, 2008), and UKMO-HadCM3 (Pope and others, 2000) simulations produced using the B1, A1B, and A2 greenhouse gas emissions scenarios.

Table 3. Mean annual growing degree days on a 5 degrees Celsius base (GDD5) anomalies, mean annual moisture index, and mean temperature of the coldest month anomalies for 2070–2099 (30-year mean) for the Fort Benning study area. Values were calculated from downscaled CCSM3 (Collins and others, 2006a), CGCM3.1(T47) (Scinocca and others, 2008), and UKMO-HadCM3 (Pope and others, 2000) coupled atmosphere-ocean general circulation model simulations produced using the B1, A1B, and A2 greenhouse gas emissions scenarios.

Model simulation	Greenhouse gas emissions scenario		
	B1	A1B	A2
Mean annual growing degree days on a 5 degrees Celsius base anomalies (percent)[1]			
CCSM3	+12	+23	+30
CGCM3.1(T47)	+16	+22	+28
UKMO-HadCM3	+25	+33	+36
Mean annual moisture index[2]			
CCSM3	0.9355	0.9273	0.9171
CGCM3.1(T47)	0.8881	0.9161	0.9281
UKMO-HadCM3	0.8804	0.8887	0.8232
Mean temperature of the coldest month anomalies (degrees Celsius)[3]			
CCSM3	+1.52	+2.23	+2.98
CGCM3.1(T47)	+1.64	+2.33	+2.74
UKMO-HadCM3	+2.92	+3.38	+2.80

[1]Growing degree day anomalies calculated by multiplying by 100 the quotient of 2070–2099 (30-year mean) GDD5 divided by 1961–1990 (30-year mean) GDD5.

[2]Moisture index calculated as actual evapotranspiration divided by potential evapotranspiration. Note that moisture index values are simulated 2070–2099 30-year mean values and not anomalies for 2070–2099.

[3]Mean temperature of the coldest month anomalies calculated as 2070–2099 (30-year mean) values minus 1961–1990 (30-year) mean values.

for the shade-intolerant broadleaved summergreen PFT was set at 0.20 to reflect the moderate fire resistance reported for species such as turkey oak (*Q. laevis*) and post oak (*Q. stellata*) (Burns and Honkala, 1990). The fire resistance parameter for the broadleaved evergreen PFT was set at 0.05 to represent the limited fire resistance for some broadleaved evergreen species, such as American holly (*Ilex opaca*) (Prasad and others, 2007).

For the LPJ-GUESS simulations, maximum nonstressed age for the needleleaved evergreen PFT was set to 400 years based on values for longleaf pine reported by Prasad and others (2007). The maximum nonstressed age for the shade-tolerant broadleaved summergreen PFT was set to 200 years, based on maximum ages reported for southern red oak (*Quercus falcata* var. falcata) (Prasad and others, 2007). The maximum nonstressed age for the shade-intolerant broadleaved summergreen PFT was set to 400 years. This value is the maximum age reported by Prasad and others (2007) for post oak (*Q. stellata*). The broadleaved evergreen PFT maximum age was set to 200 years, representing shorter-lived, frequently subcanopy species, such as American holly (Prasad and others, 2007).

Simulated Historical Vegetation

LPJ was used to simulate biome types across the entire study area. Simulated PFT foliar projective cover (FPC) for woody PFTs was used to define forest (greater than 30 percent FPC), savanna (10-30 percent FPC), and grassland (less than 10 percent FPC). The vegetation simulated by LPJ for the 20th-century was a mixed needleleaved evergreen and broadleaved evergreen and deciduous forest. This simulated vegetation corresponds well to the oak-hickory-pine forest described by Küchler (1993) as the dominant potential natural vegetation for the region. The simulated vegetation was sensitive to interannual variations in climate. For example, the 1925 and 1954 droughts in the southeastern United States were reflected in the simulated vegetation by decreases in annual net primary productivity across the study area. These droughts are recorded in Palmer Drought Severity Index (PDSI) reconstructions as PDSI values less than -1.0 (Cook and others, 2004).

Open longleaf pine forests provide good forage sites for red-cockaded woodpeckers (Van Lear and others, 2005). The birds are cavity nesters that require large diameter trees

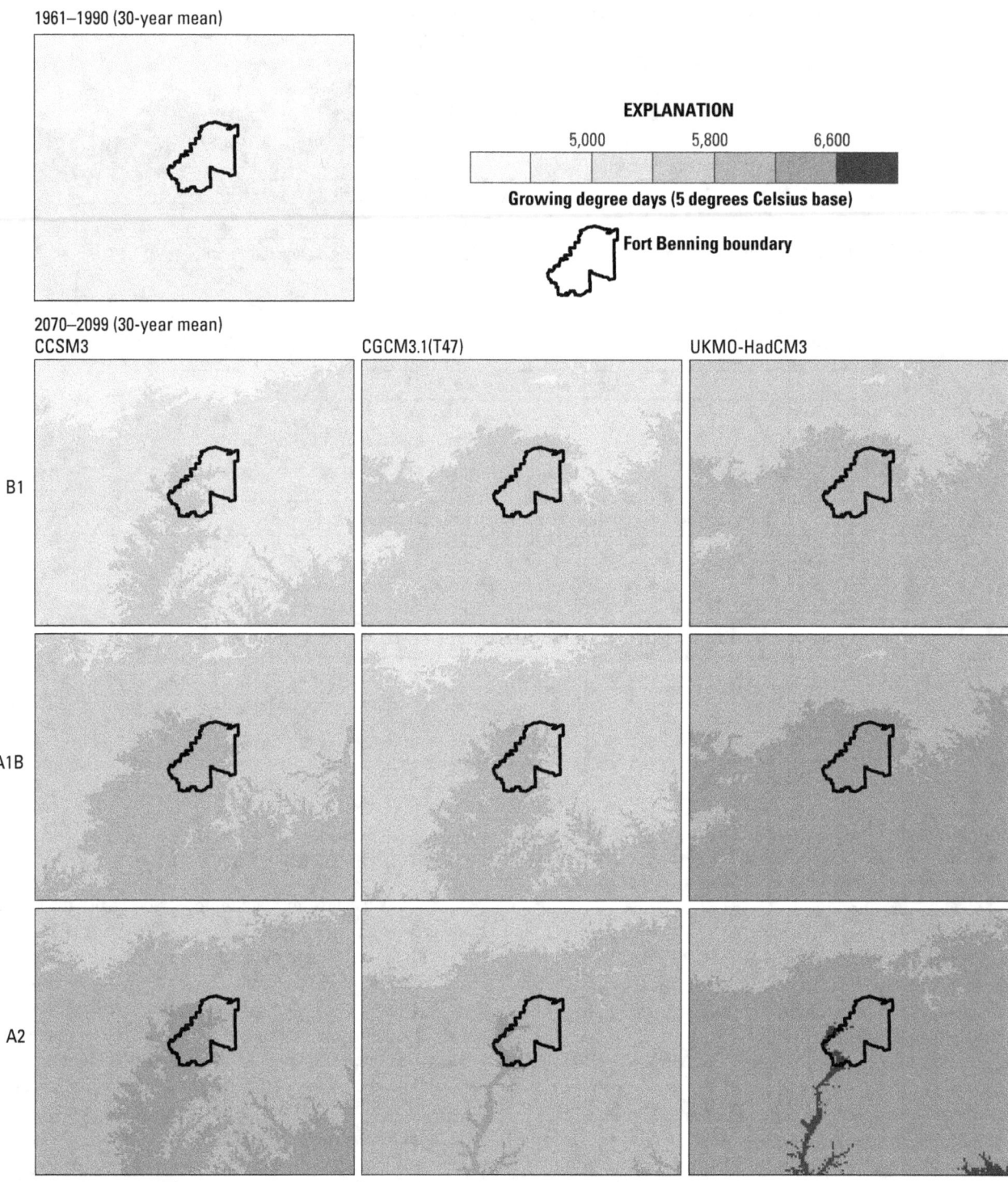

Figure 7.   Mean annual growing degree days (on a 5 degrees Celsius base) for the Fort Benning study area and the boundary of Fort Benning (black line). Top row: 1961–1990 (30-year mean) mean annual growing degree days (on a 5 degrees Celsius base) calculated from downscaled CRU CL 2.0 (New and others, 2002) and CRU TS 2.1 (Mitchell and Jones, 2005) data. Bottom rows: 2070–2099 (30-year mean) mean annual growing degree days (on a 5 degrees Celsius base) calculated from downscaled CCSM3 (Collins and others, 2006a), CGCM3.1(T47) (Scinocca and others, 2008), and UKMO-HadCM3 (Pope and others, 2000) simulations produced using the B1, A1B, and A2 greenhouse gas emissions scenarios.

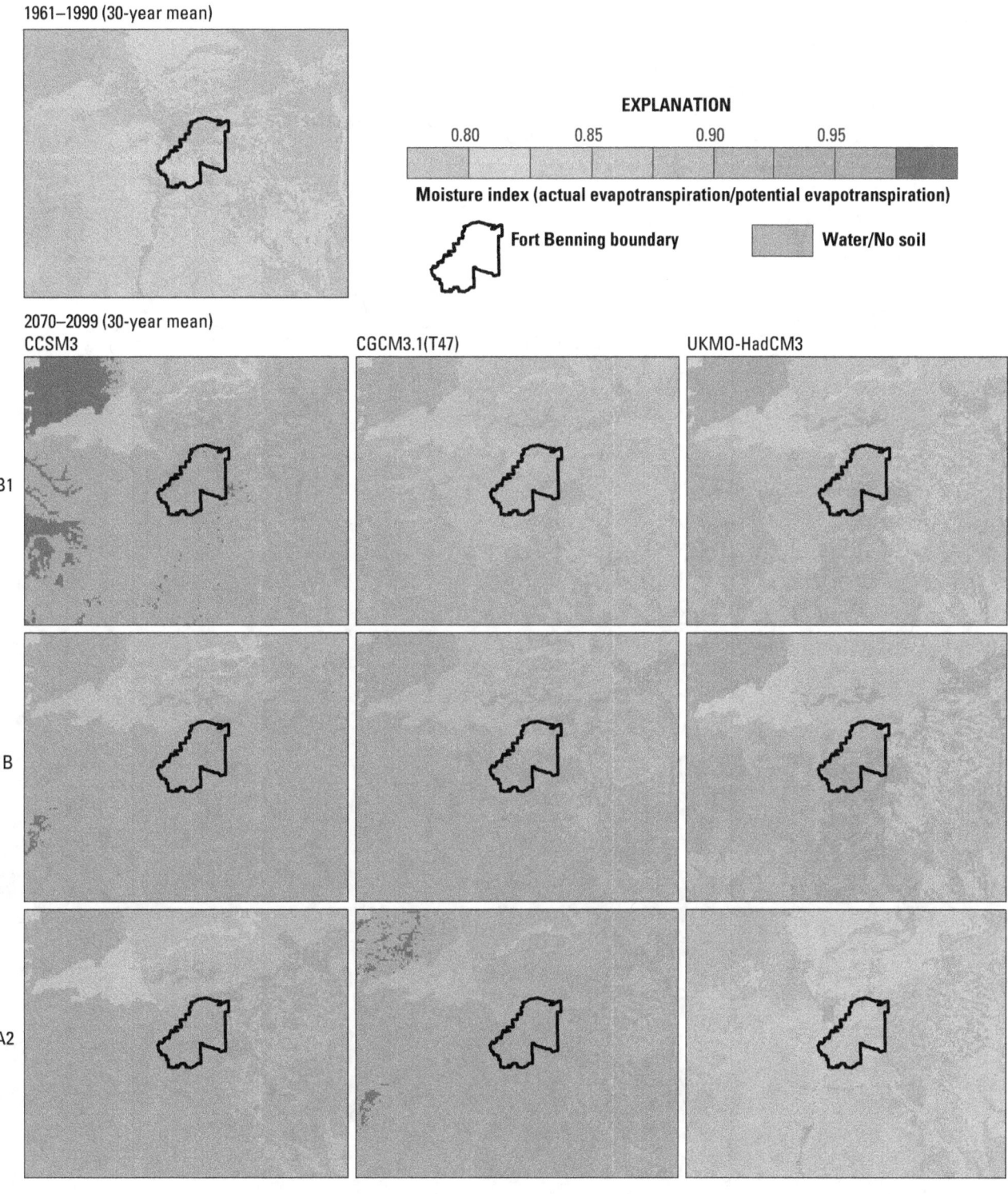

Figure 8. Mean annual moisture index (actual evapotranspiration divided by potential evapotranspiration) for the Fort Benning study area and the boundary of Fort Benning (black line). Top row: 1961–1990 (30-year mean) mean annual moisture index calculated from downscaled CRU CL 2.0 (New and others, 2002) and CRU TS 2.1 (Mitchell and Jones, 2005) data. Bottom rows: 2070–2099 (30-year mean) mean annual moisture index calculated from downscaled CCSM3 (Collins and others, 2006a), CGCM3.1(T47) (Scinocca and others, 2008), and UKMO-HadCM3 (Pope and others, 2000) simulations produced using the B1, A1B, and A2 greenhouse gas emissions scenarios.

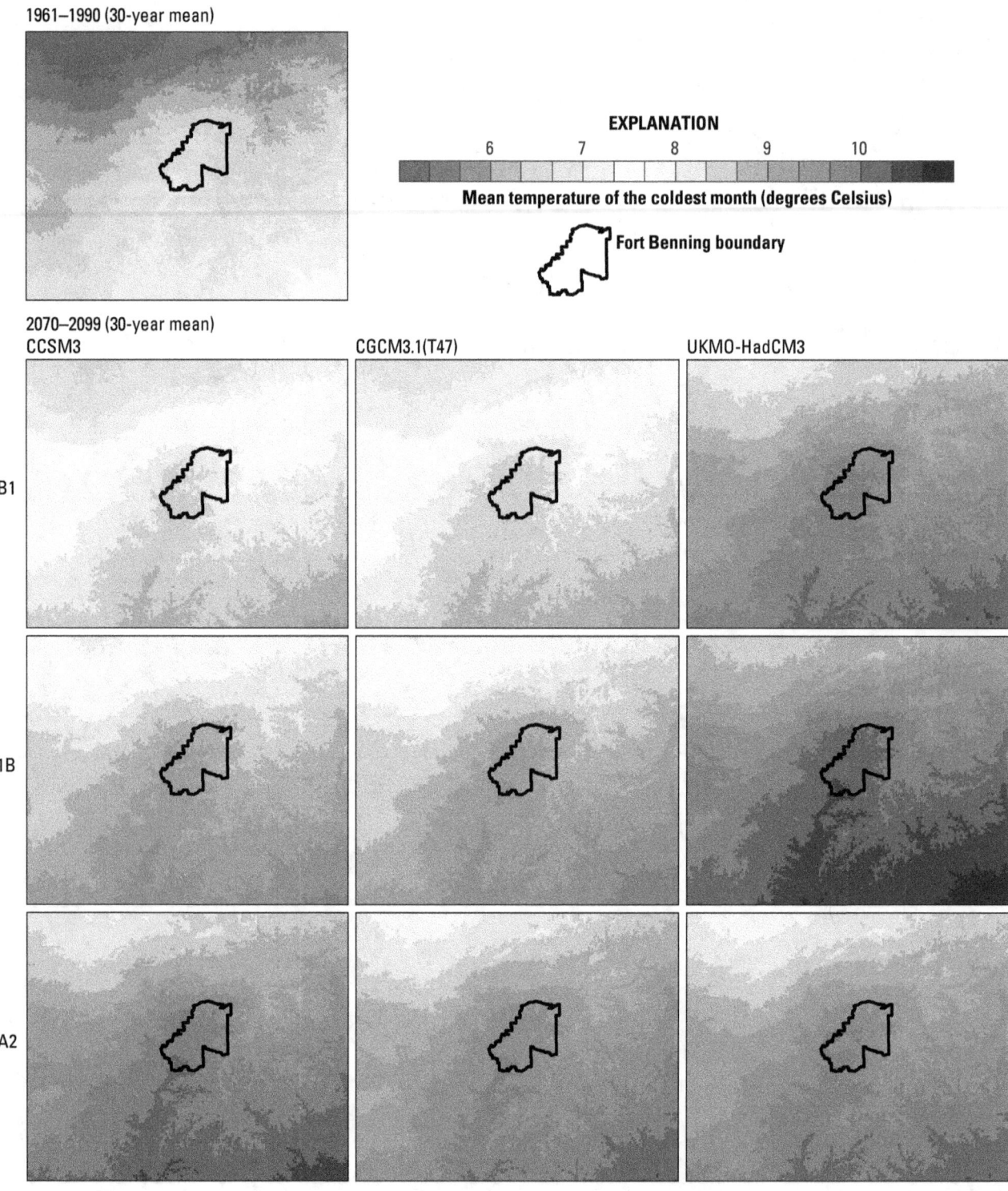

Figure 9. Mean temperature of the coldest month (degrees Celsius) for the Fort Benning study area and the boundary of Fort Benning (black line). Top row: 1961–1990 (30-year mean) mean temperature of the coldest month calculated from downscaled CRU CL 2.0 (New and others, 2002) and CRU TS 2.1 (Mitchell and Jones, 2005) data. Bottom rows: 2070–2099 (30-year mean) mean temperature of the coldest month calculated from downscaled CCSM3 (Collins and others, 2006a), CGCM3.1(T47) (Scinocca and others, 2008), and UKMO-HadCM3 (Pope and others, 2000) simulations produced using the B1, A1B, and A2 greenhouse gas emissions scenarios.

for nest sites (Rudolph and Conner, 1991; Butler and Tappe, 2008). To project potential future changes to these components of red-cockaded woodpecker habitat, LPJ-GUESS was used to simulate basal area and tree density for the needleleaved evergreen PFT. Holder (2000) examined five *P. palustris* sites in the southeastern United States in stands ranging in age from 27–71 years old and found stand densities of 246–1,000 trees per hectare (ha^{-1}) for trees more than 5.0 centimeters (cm) in diameter at breast height. Varner and Kush (2004) summarized data from a number of studies that report old-growth longleaf forests and savannas with basal areas of 12–35 square meters per hectare (m^2 ha^{-1}) and stand densities of 130–400 trees ha^{-1}. LPJ-GUESS simulated a 1961–1990 (30-year mean) basal area of 35 m^2 ha^{-1} and a density of 458 trees ha^{-1} for needleleaved evergreen PFT individuals greater than 20 years old. The simulated basal area value falls within the range of observed values while the simulated density value is greater than observed values (Varner and Kush 2004).

Simulated Future Vegetation

LPJ simulated a mixed needleleaf and broadleaf forest for the study area under all nine model and emissions scenario combinations through 2099 with no major changes in vegetation. Other vegetation modeling studies, using different potential future climate data and emissions scenarios, report generally similar results for the same region (Solomon, 1986; Bachelet and others, 2008; Lenihan and others, 2008).

LPJ-GUESS likewise projected no major changes in vegetation across the study area, simulating the continued persistence of needleleaved evergreen forest. Projected needleleaved evergreen PFT basal area was approximately

35 m^2 ha^{-1} under all nine AOGCM and emissions scenario combinations for 2070–2099 (30-year mean) for trees more than 20 years old (table 4). These values matched the 1961–1990 (30-year mean) basal area for needleleaved evergreen PFT trees more than 20 years old simulated for the study area. Simulated needleleaved evergreen PFT tree density ranged from 450.3 trees ha^{-1} under the B1 emissions scenario to 453.5 trees ha^{-1} under the A2 emissions scenario for 2070–2099 (30-year mean) for trees more than 20 years old (table 4). These density values were slightly lower than the simulated 1961–1990 (30-year mean) needleleaved evergreen PFT density of 458 trees ha^{-1}.

The projected future PFT basal area and density values do not vary much among the nine model and emissions scenario combinations (table 4). This agreement is a result, in part, of the similar climate that PFTs experience under all nine AOGCM and emissions scenario combinations through the middle of the 21st century. All of the vegetation simulations use identical climate data for the 800-year spin-up period and for the 20th century. In the 21st century, the three emissions scenarios produce similar changes in temperature and precipitation through the middle of the 21st century, and it is only after this point that the future climate projections display substantial differences (Meehl and others, 2007b).

Although mean annual temperatures are projected to increase under all nine future climate simulations, the projected temperature changes may remain suitable for longleaf pine. Projected future mean annual temperature increases for the study area range from 1.58 °C under the CCSM3 B1 simulation to 4.66 °C under the UKMO-HadCM3 A2 simulation. Even in the case of the largest mean annual temperature change projected under the UKMO-HadCM3

Table 4. Mean basal area (square meters per hectare) and density (individuals per hectare) of needleleaved evergreen plant functional type (PFT) individuals greater than 20 years old for 2070–2099 (30-year mean) as simulated by LPJ-GUESS (Smith and others, 2001) for the Fort Benning study area. LPJ-GUESS was run using climate data from downscaled CCSM3 (Collins and others, 2006a), CGCM3.1(T47) (Scinocca and others, 2008), and UKMO-HadCM3 (Pope and others, 2000) coupled atmosphere-ocean general circulation model simulations produced using the B1, A1B, and A2 greenhouse gas emissions scenarios.

Needleleaved evergreen PFT individuals greater than 20 years old	Greenhouse gas emissions scenario		
	B1	A1B	A2
Basal area (square meters per hectare)			
CCSM3	35.3	35.5	35.5
CGCM3.1(T47)	35.1	35.5	35.3
UKMO-HadCM3	35.1	35.5	35.2
Density (individuals per hectare)			
CCSM3	451.5	453.2	453.5
CGCM3.1(T47)	451.6	453.2	451.7
UKMO-HadCM3	450.3	453.2	453.0

A2 simulation, the mean annual temperature across the study area would be 22.36 °C (2070–2099 30-year mean), which is within the range of historical mean annual temperatures experienced by longleaf pine in the southeastern United States (Thompson and others, 1999).

Implications of Future Climate and Vegetation Changes for Species

The vegetation simulations for the Fort Benning study area indicate that projected future climate may remain suitable for both the pine and mixed pine-hardwood forests and woodlands that are present across the region. If these vegetation types persist, they could continue to provide habitat for the many species that depend on them. Longleaf pine forests support particularly high levels of biodiversity (Mitchell and others, 2006) and they provide habitat for a large number of mammal, bird, herpetofauna, insect, and plant species, including many species that are federally listed (Van Lear and others, 2005). Maintaining longleaf pine forests in the future, along with other important habitat types, will be critical for the successful management of many species in the region.

The vegetation simulations, however, must be interpreted with caution. They simulate only some aspects of the information that is needed to understand potential future vegetation changes for the study area. For example, future climate changes could alter the distributions of insect pests and diseases, such as southeastern pine beetle (*Dendroctonus frontalis*), which could significantly affect forests in the region (Gan, 2004). Insect and disease dynamics were not included in our vegetation simulations. Future changes in extreme climate events, such as extreme temperatures that last for multiple days producing drought stress, could also significantly affect vegetation (for example, Pederson and others, 2008), but these extreme events may not be captured by the monthly climate data used in this study. Similarly, some of the species-specific responses to disturbance, such as root sprouting exhibited by some oak species (Del Tredici, 2001), are not simulated in the vegetation models. Finally, although the vegetation models simulate the persistence of both pine forests and mixed pine and hardwood forests, the models were not set up to simulate all of the individual tree species that occur in the region's forests. Both the type and frequency of plant species in the study area may change under future climate conditions.

Among the many species in the Fort Benning study area that would be affected by vegetation changes is the red-cockaded woodpecker, a federally listed endangered species that is endemic to southeastern pine forests (U.S. Fish and Wildlife Service, 2003). The red-cockaded woodpecker is a cavity nester, and it relies on pine stands for both nesting sites and foraging habitat. Although the red-cockaded woodpecker will occupy cavities in a number of different pine species, such as loblolly pine (*Pinus taeda*) and shortleaf pine (*P. echinata*), they prefer cavities in longleaf pine trees for nesting sites (Rudolph and Conner, 1991). Red-cockaded woodpeckers

preferentially create cavities in older trees, frequently choosing among the oldest available trees within their territories (Rudolph and Conner, 1991). Land-use activities, however, have reduced longleaf pine forests and woodlands in the southeastern United States to a small percentage of their spatial extent prior to Euro-American settlement (Landers and others, 1995). Today, many of the existing longleaf pine stands in the study area are relatively young as a result of past logging and agricultural activities in the region (Mitchell and others, 2006; Maloney and others, 2008). The LPJ-GUESS vegetation simulations indicate that pine forests could persist in the study area through the end of the century. If existing longleaf pine stands are protected, already established younger age classes of trees may be able to mature into age and size classes that provide suitable red-cockaded woodpecker habitat.

Longleaf pine forests are fire-dependent systems (Mitchell and others, 2006; although see also Schnurr and Collins, 2007). Past fire suppression across the Fort Benning study area has allowed broadleaved vegetation to become established in pine forests (Collins and others, 2006c) leading to increased fuel load and intensity of fires (Van Lear and others, 2005). Continued prescribed burning of remnant longleaf pine stands may help to maintain longleaf pine forests, although significant tree mortality from fires may occur in stands where fire previously has been suppressed (Varner and others, 2005; Varner and others, 2007). With the exception of large stand-replacing fires that might result from fuel buildup following fire suppression, increased fire frequency as a result of climate change will likely improve red-cockaded woodpecker habitat. Frequent fires also may be important in maintaining depressional wetland habitat in the region by removing vegetation (Kirkman and others, 1998; Martin and Kirkman, 2009).

In addition to fire, future changes in the frequency and severity of storms could affect red-cockaded woodpecker habitat. Engstrom and Evans (1990) reported significant mortality of red-cockaded woodpecker cavity trees in Georgia following hurricanes in 1985. Some studies indicate that hurricane wind speeds could increase in the future (Meehl and others, 2007b), which could increase damage to cavity trees.

Among the other species found in open longleaf pine forests are gopher tortoises (*Gopherus polyphemus*) (Guyer and others, 2006). Gopher tortoises generally occur in areas with sandy soils that are well-drained and provide suitable conditions for digging burrows (Diemer, 1986). Gopher tortoises use their burrows as thermal refuges when above ground temperatures are too warm (Wilson and others, 1994). The use of burrows to escape high temperatures is important particularly for juveniles (Wilson and others, 1994) and thus, burrows in the study area may be used increasingly as air temperatures increase in the future. Gopher tortoises also prefer areas with open canopies that allow sunlight to reach the ground. Direct sunlight is important for a number of reasons, including allowing the tortoises to meet their thermal requirements for daily activity, providing sunlit nest sites, and increasing the cover of the herbs and grasses the tortoises feed on (Mushinsky and McCoy, 1994). Future climate changes that decrease the quantity of herbs and grasses available in late summer and early fall could lead to earlier and(or) increased dispersal of tortoises from breeding colonies (McRae and others, 1981).

There are a number of species in the Fort Benning study area that use aquatic habitats, including the American alligator (*Alligator mississippiensis*), the wood stork (*Mycteria americana*), and the gopher frog (*Rana capito*). Rivers, streams, ponds, and wetlands all occur within the study area. These sites provide aquatic habitats that may be maintained by a variety of water sources, each of which may be more or less sensitive to projected future changes in temperature and precipitation. For example, ephemeral wetlands that are maintained by the frequency and magnitude of precipitation events may be quite sensitive to future changes in precipitation and temperature regimes. At the other end of the spectrum, the Chattahoochee River, which flows through the study area, has numerous dams along its channel upstream from the study area that are managed for recreation, power, navigation, flood control, and fish and wildlife habitat (Richter and others, 2003). It may be possible to mitigate some of the potential effects of future climate change on river flows by managing the timing and magnitude of water releases from these upstream dams.

American alligators are listed as threatened according to the "similarity of appearance" provision of the 1973 Endangered Species Act (U.S. Fish and Wildlife Service, 1987). In the Fort Benning study area they are at the northern edge of their range (Lance, 2003) and mortality from cold temperatures are a factor limiting their northward expansion (Brisbin and others, 1982). They experience lethargy and torpor at temperatures below approximately 16 °C (Lance, 2003). Projected future temperature increases in the study area would allow American alligators to remain active for a longer period of time during the year and might allow them to expand their range northward. Increased air temperatures may affect nest incubation temperatures (Chabreck, 1973), although Chabreck (1973) reported no direct relation between nest and air temperatures. Future temperature and precipitation changes that lead to decreases in water level and pond areas could lead to increased predation on nests (Hunt and Ogden, 1991). Alligators that occupy water bodies with managed water levels, such as the Chattahoochee River, could have the effects of climate change on their aquatic habitats mitigated by adjusting water management practices.

Gopher frogs are another species in the study area that use aquatic habitats. They tend to breed in ephemeral upland ponds (Richter and others, 2001). At Fort Benning, breeding areas include both natural ponds and wetlands as well as ponds constructed as wildlife watering holes, all of which may dry out for periods of time during the year (J. Neufeldt, U.S. Army Conservation Branch, Fort Benning, pers. comm.). Projected increases in temperature for the study area could increase both direct evaporation of water and the evapotranspiration of water by plants. This potential loss of water could lead to an increase in the frequency and duration of the periods during the year when breeding sites are dry. For breeding sites that are maintained by direct precipitation, the potential effect of increased temperatures will depend on the accompanying frequency and magnitude of precipitation events.

In addition to reptiles and amphibians, there are many bird species that use aquatic and riparian habitats across the study area. For example, the United States breeding populations of wood storks are federally listed as endangered (U.S. Fish and Wildlife Service, 1984). Wood storks are summer migrants at Fort Benning (M. Thornton, U.S. Army Conservation Branch, Fort Benning, pers. comm.) although there are no known nesting colonies in the study area (Brooks and Dean, 2008). Wood storks use aquatic habitats for foraging, and the timing and height of water levels significantly can affect the availability of important prey. Lower water levels may concentrate prey species that provide food for nestlings (Bryan and Robinette, 2008). Higher water levels may disperse prey, which can lead to decreased breeding success (Bryan and Robinette, 2008). Severe storms can destroy wood stork nests and kill nestlings (Coulter and Bryan, 1995). Projected future changes in the frequency and(or) severity of storms (Meehl and others, 2007b), particularly during the breeding season, could affect wood stork reproductive success.

Many plant species occur across the Fort Benning study area. Kirkman and others (2001) ascribe the high plant diversity in longleaf pine forests to the presence of numerous perennial plant species that are adapted to fire. The mixed deciduous forests in the study area also provide important habitat for plant species. Relict trillium (*Trillium reliquum*) is an ephemeral herb in the southeastern United States that is federally listed as an endangered species (U.S. Fish and Wildlife Service, 1988). It occurs in mixed deciduous forests, where it emerges from approximately February to April and is dormant the rest of the year (Case and Case, 1997). Relict trilliums are threatened by habitat loss (Heckel and Leege, 2007) although recent genetic analyses indicate that the existing disjunct populations in the southeastern United States have been isolated from one another since before Euro-American settlement (Gonzales and Hamrick, 2005). At this time, not enough is known about the ecology and physiology of relict trilliums to project potential climate change effects on the species.

In addition to relict trillium, there are many other herbaceous plant species, such as Georgia rockcress (*Arabis georgiana*), that are species of concern in the region. Georgia rockcress is listed as threatened by the Georgia Department of Natural Resources and is a candidate for federal listing (Patrick and others, 1995). As with relict trillium, relatively little is known about its physiology and ecology, making it difficult to assess the potential effects future climate change may have on the species. For many herbaceous and understory plant species, maintaining substrate or overstory conditions may help the species to persist in the future. In many cases, factors other than climate change, such as habitat loss resulting from land-use changes, are more immediate threats to a species' persistence (Sala and others, 2000). In the case of Georgia rockcress, Patrick and others (1995) list controlling exotic plant species, particularly Japanese honeysuckle (*Lonicera japonica*), as an important management activity.

Fort Hood Study Area

Site Description

The Fort Hood study area (22,282 km²) is located in central Texas (fig. 2) and is centered on the Fort Hood Military Reservation. The area lies at the edge of the Edwards Plateau with estimated elevations of the study area grid points ranging from approximately 87 m to approximately 519 m above sea level (Gesch and others, 2002). The study area is in the shortgrass steppe and prairies and savannas ecoregions defined by Bailey (1997). Juniper-oak savanna and Blackland prairie are the dominant potential natural vegetation for the region according to Küchler (1993). Woody vegetation across the site includes Ashe's juniper (*Juniperus ashei*), mesquite (*Prosopis glandulosa*), and a number of oak species such as Texas live oak (*Quercus fusiformis*) and shin oak (*Quercus sinuata* var. *breviloba*) (Bailey and Thompson, 2007). Additional studies describing the vegetation at Fort Hood include Johnson (1982).

Climate

The estimated 1961–1990 30-year mean temperatures for the Fort Hood study area are 18.7 °C annually, 18.7 °C in spring (March–May), 27.9 °C in summer (June–August), 19.6 °C in fall (September–November) and 8.6 °C in winter (December–February). The estimated 1961–1990 30-year mean precipitation for the study area is 812 mm annually, 243 mm in spring (March–May), 183 mm in summer (June–August), 232 mm in fall (September–November), and 154 mm in winter (December–February). The 1961–1990 30-year mean bioclimatic values are 5,014 GDD5, 0.60 for the moisture index (AET/PET), and 6.5 °C for the mean temperature of the coldest month.

Projected future mean annual temperature changes for the region for 2070–2099 (30-year mean) range from an increase of 1.86 °C simulated by CCSM3 under the B1 emissions scenario to 5.21 °C simulated by UKMO-HadCM3 under the A2 emissions scenario (table 5, fig. 10). Projected future mean annual precipitation changes for the region for 2070–2099 (30-year mean) range from a 5 percent decrease simulated by CCSM3 under the A2 emissions scenario to an 18 percent increase simulated by CGCM3.1(T47) under the A2 emissions scenario (table 5, fig. 11).

GDD5 values are projected to increase by the end of the century under all nine AOGCM and emissions scenario combinations (table 6, fig. 12). The moisture index (AET/PET)

is projected to decrease from 0.60 (1961–1990 30-year mean) under the CCSM3 A2 and UKMO-HadCM3 B1 and A2 simulations but to increase under the other six AOGCM and emissions scenario combinations (table 6, fig. 13). Mean temperature of the coldest month increases under all nine AOGCM and emissions scenario combinations (table 6, fig. 14) with increases ranging from 0.88 °C simulated by CCSM3 under the B1 emissions scenario to 4.22 °C simulated by CCSM3 under the A2 emissions scenario (2070–2099 30-year mean).

Vegetation

LPJ was used to simulate vegetation changes for the entire Fort Hood study area. For a smaller area surrounding Fort Hood (fig. 2), LPJ-GUESS was used to simulate changes in foliar projective cover for broadleaved woody PFTs that provide important habitat for nesting birds, such as the black-capped vireo (*Vireo atricapilla*), one of the species of management concern at Fort Hood (Tazik and others, 1993b).

Vegetation Model Parameters

For the LPJ simulations we used the model parameters described in tables 1 and 2 of Sitch and others (2003) except for fire resistance values. Fire resistance in LPJ for the evergreen needleleaved PFT was set to 0.15 to represent the low fire resistance of Ashe's juniper (Wink and Wright, 1973). The fire resistance parameters for the broadleaved PFTs were set at 0.12 to represent the relatively low fire resistance reported for some broadleaved species (Prasad and others, 2007).

For the LPJ-GUESS simulations, maximum nonstressed age for the needleleaved evergreen PFT was set to 300 years. This age was based on values for eastern redcedar (*Juniperus virginiana*) reported by Prasad and others (2007) in the absence of data for Ashe's juniper. The maximum nonstressed age for both the shade-tolerant and shade-intolerant broadleaved summergreen PFTs was set to 400 years to represent the maximum ages reported for species such as post oak (*Q. stellata*) (Prasad and others, 2007). The broadleaved evergreen PFT maximum age was set to 400 years from data for live oak (*Q. virginiana*) as a surrogate for Texas live oak (Prasad and others, 2007). In LPJ-GUESS the fire resistance parameter for all woody PFTs was set to 0.12.

Simulated Historical Vegetation

Historical vegetation for the Fort Hood study area consisted of grasslands and savannas with denser tree cover found in more mesic areas, such as along riparian corridors (Reemts and Hansen, 2007). When the LPJ and LPJ-GUESS simulations included fire, the simulated 20th century vegetation for the Fort Hood study area matched the general description of savanna as the potential natural vegetation for the region (Fowler and Dunlap, 1986). LPJ simulated

Table 5. Mean annual and seasonal temperature (degrees Celsius) and precipitation (percent) anomalies for 2070–2099 (30-year mean) for the Fort Hood study area. Anomalies were calculated from downscaled CCSM3 (Collins and others, 2006a), CGCM3.1(T47) (Scinocca and others, 2008), and UKMO-HadCM3 (Pope and others, 2000) coupled atmosphere-ocean general circulation model simulations produced using the B1, A1B, and A2 greenhouse gas emissions scenarios.

| Model simulation | Greenhouse gas emissions scenario | | | | | |
| | B1 | | A1B | | A2 | |
	Temperature[1] (degrees Celsius)	Precipitation[2] (percent)	Temperature[1] (degrees Celsius)	Precipitation[2] (percent)	Temperature[1] (degrees Celsius)	Precipitation[2] (percent)
			Annual			
CCSM3	+1.86	+8	+3.43	+1	+4.55	-5
CGCM3.1(T47)	+1.96	+9	+2.80	+15	+3.59	+18
UKMO-HadCM3	+3.64	-3	+4.57	+5	+5.21	-2
			December–February			
CCSM3	+1.76	+6	+3.40	-3	+4.68	-15
CGCM3.1(T47)	+1.76	-8	+2.53	-10	+3.41	-11
UKMO-HadCM3	+3.51	-4	+4.11	+3	+3.58	+3
			March–May			
CCSM3	+1.83	+13	+3.11	+17	+3.94	+23
CGCM3.1(T47)	+1.92	+2	+3.15	+5	+3.69	+21
UKMO-HadCM3	+3.20	-5	+4.19	-2	+5.38	-21
			June–August			
CCSM3	+1.99	-3	+3.45	-17	+4.58	-21
CGCM3.1(T47)	+1.95	+11	+2.26	+43	+3.46	+15
UKMO-HadCM3	+4.42	-16	+5.92	-22	+6.72	-11
			September–November			
CCSM3	+1.85	+14	+3.77	-1	+4.98	-14
CGCM3.1(T47)	+2.21	+24	+3.24	+20	+3.81	+35
UKMO-HadCM3	+3.43	+8	+4.07	+36	+5.18	+19

[1]Temperature anomalies were calculated as 2070–2099 (30-year mean) simulated temperature minus 1961–1990 (30-year mean) simulated temperature.

[2]Precipitation anomalies were calculated by multiplying by 100 the quotient of 2070–2099 (30-year mean) simulated precipitation divided by 1961–1990 (30-year mean) simulated precipitation.

approximately 40 percent grass PFT foliar projective cover and approximately 57 percent woody PFT foliar projective cover for 1961–1990 (30-year mean) for the study area. LPJ-GUESS simulated approximately 67 percent grass PFT foliar projective cover and less than 5 percent woody PFT foliar projective cover for the study area over the same time period. The differences in the relative amounts of woody and grass vegetation simulated by the two models may reflect differences in the way the two models parameterize individual-level processes (Smith and others, 2001). Smith and others (2001) noted that, relative to both empirical data and LPJ-GUESS simulations, LPJ overestimates woody vegetation abundance compared to grass abundance in areas with seasonal water deficits.

Black-capped vireos prefer woody vegetation less than 2.5 m in height for nest sites (fig. 15; Bailey and Thompson, 2007). To approximate this height class of vegetation, we used simulated needleleaved evergreen PFT data for individuals less than 25 years old as simulated by LPJ-GUESS. This age threshold was based on growth rates of 0.1 m year[-1] reported by Kroll (1980) and McLemore and others (2004). For broadleaved summergreen and evergreen PFTs we used data for individuals less than 20 years old based on Tazik and others' (1993a) observation that vireo habitat was present 3-5 years after a fire and remained good vireo habitat for the subsequent 20–25 years.

Simulated Future Vegetation

LPJ simulations that include fire produce a mix of needleleaved evergreen, broadleaved summergreen and evergreen, and grass PFTs under projected future climate conditions. The different AOGCM and emissions scenario combinations produce a range of vegetation responses. Grass PFT foliar projective cover is simulated to increase from 1961–1990 (30-year mean) to 2070–2099 (30-year mean) under four of the nine AOGCM and emissions scenario combinations and woody PFT foliar projective cover increases

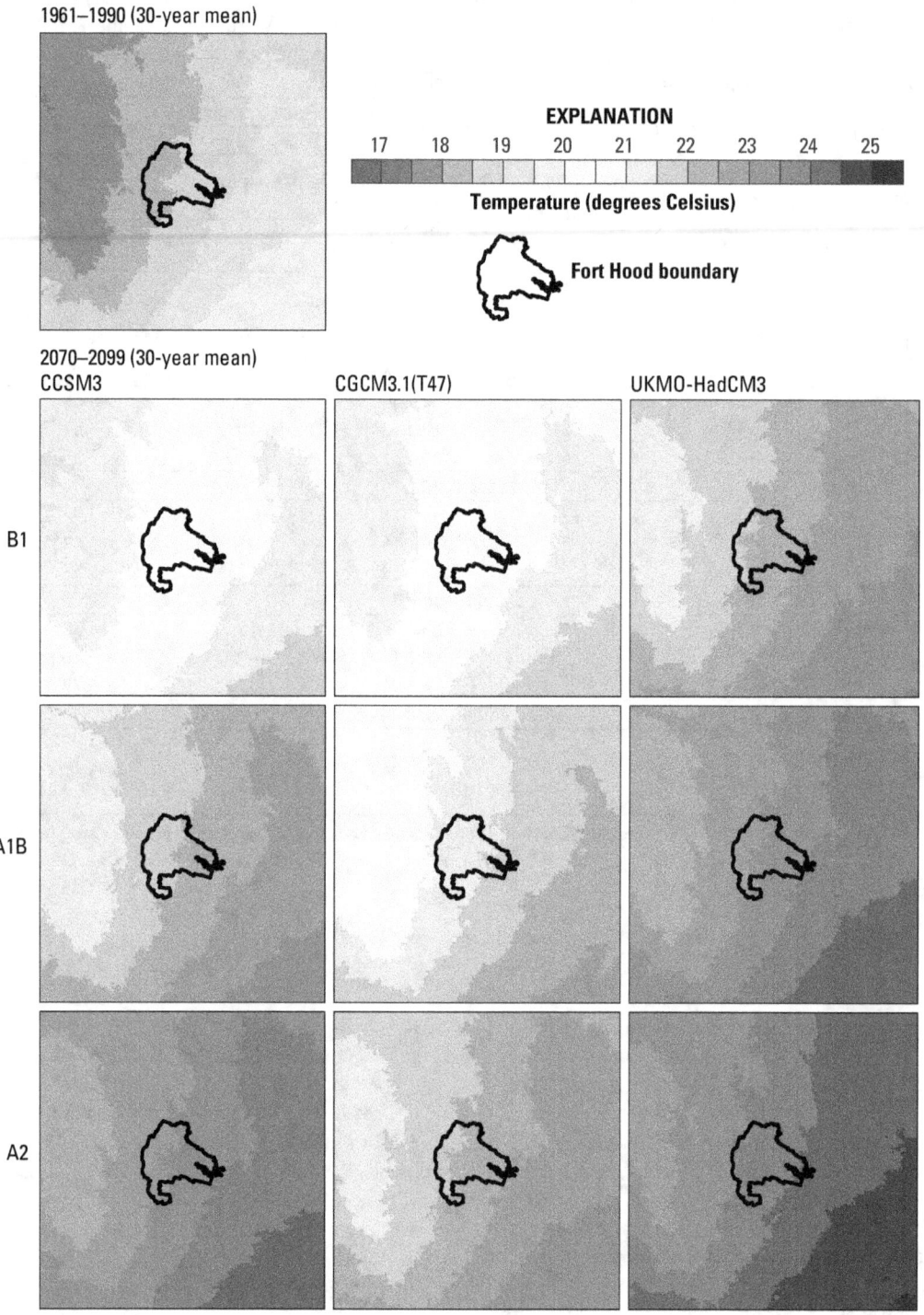

Figure 10.   Mean annual temperature (degrees Celsius) for the Fort Hood study area and the boundary of Fort Hood (black line). Top row: 1961-1990 (30-year mean) mean annual temperature calculated from downscaled CRU CL 2.0 (New and others, 2002) and CRU TS 2.1 (Mitchell and Jones, 2005) data. Bottom rows: 2070-2099 (30-year mean) mean annual temperature calculated from downscaled CCSM3 (Collins and others, 2006a), CGCM3.1(T47) (Scinocca and others, 2008), and UKMO-HadCM3 (Pope and others, 2000) simulations produced using the B1, A1B, and A2 greenhouse gas emissions scenarios.

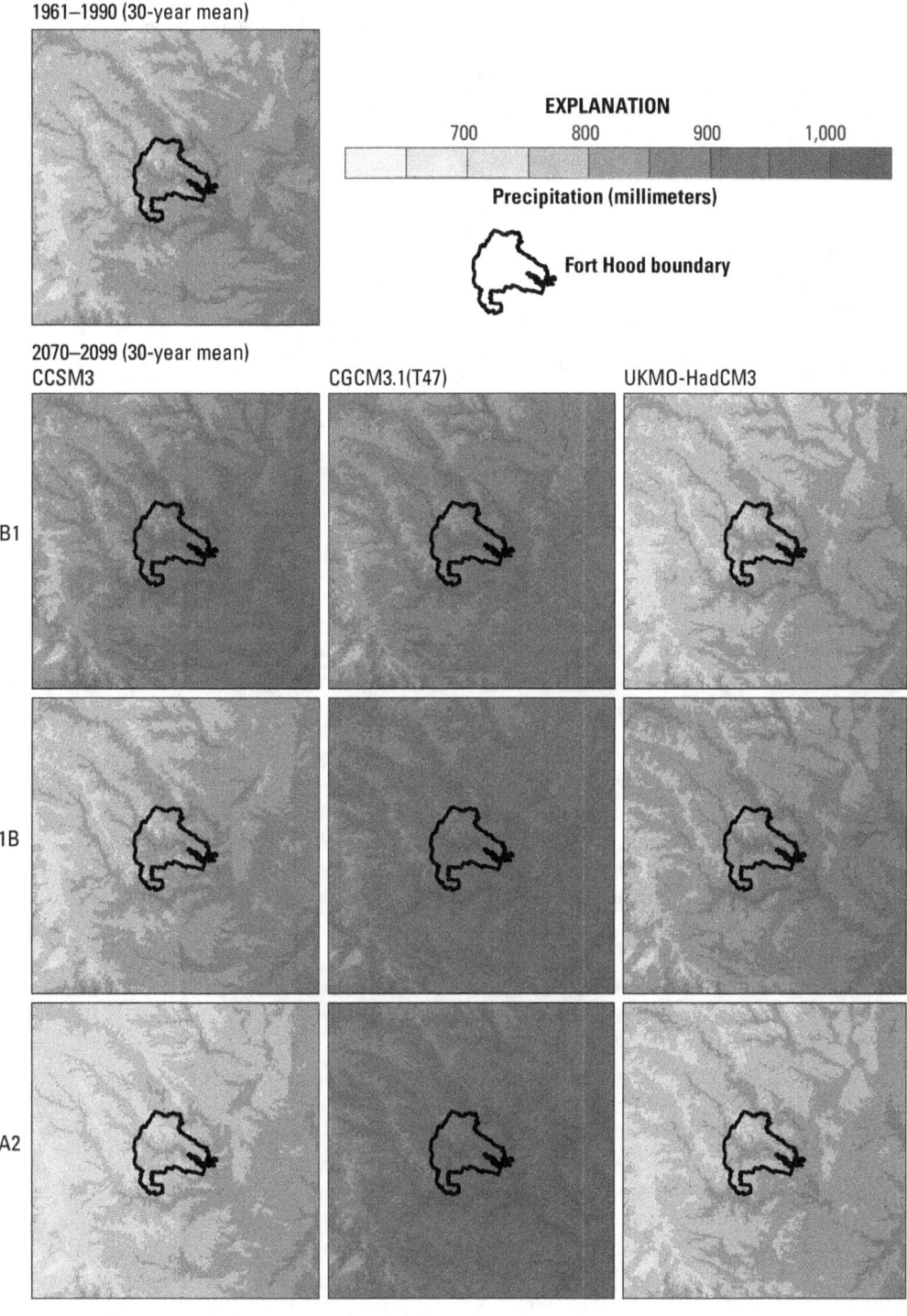

Figure 11.   Mean total annual precipitation (millimeters) for the Fort Hood study area and the boundary of Fort Hood (black line). Top row: 1961–1990 (30-year mean) mean total annual precipitation calculated from downscaled CRU CL 2.0 (New and others, 2002) and CRU TS 2.1 (Mitchell and Jones, 2005) data. Bottom rows: 2070–2099 (30-year mean) mean total annual precipitation calculated from downscaled CCSM3 (Collins and others, 2006a), CGCM3.1(T47) (Scinocca and others, 2008), and UKMO-HadCM3 (Pope and others, 2000) simulations produced using the B1, A1B, and A2 greenhouse gas emissions scenarios.

Table 6. Mean annual growing degree days on a 5 degrees Celsius base (GDD5) anomalies, mean annual moisture index, and mean temperature of the coldest month anomalies for 2070–2099 (30-year mean) for the Fort Hood study area. Values were calculated from downscaled CCSM3 (Collins and others, 2006a), CGCM3.1(T47) (Scinocca and others, 2008), and UKMO-HadCM3 (Pope and others, 2000) coupled atmosphere-ocean general circulation model simulations produced using the B1, A1B, and A2 greenhouse gas emissions scenarios.

Model simulation	Greenhouse gas emissions scenario		
	B1	**A1B**	**A2**
Mean annual growing degree days on a 5 degrees Celsius base anomalies (percent)[1]			
CCSM3	+13	+25	+33
CGCM3.1(T47)	+14	+20	+26
UKMO-HadCM3	+26	+33	+38
Mean annual moisture index (AET/PET)[2]			
CCSM3	0.6870	0.6252	0.5813
CGCM3.1(T47)	0.6915	0.7435	0.7255
UKMO-HadCM3	0.5769	0.6001	0.5334
Mean temperature of the coldest month anomalies (degrees Celsius)[3]			
CCSM3	+0.88	+2.65	+4.22
CGCM3.1(T47)	+1.73	+2.44	+3.26
UKMO-HadCM3	+3.47	+4.05	+3.52

[1]Growing degree day anomalies calculated by multiplying by 100 the quotient of 2070–2099 (30-year mean) GDD5 divided by 1961–1990 (30-year mean) GDD5.

[2]Moisture index calculated as actual evapotranspiration divided by potential evapotranspiration. Note that moisture index values are simulated 2070–2099 30-year mean values and not anomalies for 2070–2099.

[3]Mean temperature of the coldest month anomalies calculated as 2070–2099 (30-year mean) values minus 1961–1990 (30-year) mean values.

under a different four AOGCM and emissions scenario combinations, with one AOGCM and emissions scenario combination (UKMO-HadCM3 A1B) simulating slight decreases in both grass and woody PFT foliar projective cover (table 7). LPJ-GUESS simulations produce the same mix of PFTs under projected future climates, with fire playing an important role in determining the relative amounts of woody and grass PFTs. When fires are simulated, the foliar projective cover of the grass PFT increases to approximately 65 percent and woody PFTs are reduced to less than 5 percent foliar projective cover under all nine AOGCM and emissions scenario combinations. The low occurrence of trees in the LPJ-GUESS simulations that included fire made it difficult to use these simulations to assess the potential future change to woody vegetation used for nesting by black-capped vireos. To simulate potential effects of climate on woody vegetation, a second set of LPJ-GUESS vegetation simulations were run with fire turned off in the model. These simulations provided information on the response of woody vegetation to future climate changes and atmospheric CO_2 concentrations in the absence of fire. If fires are suppressed in the LPJ-GUESS simulations, the foliar projective cover of grass decreases to approximately 10 percent while woody PFT foliar projective cover increases to approximately 46 percent under all nine AOGCM and emissions scenario combinations for 2070–2099 (30-year mean). For broadleaved PFT individuals less than

20 years old, the suppression of fires approximately doubles the foliar projective cover simulated by LPJ-GUESS under all nine AOGCM and emissions scenario combinations for 2070–2099 (30-year mean; table 8).

Implications of Future Climate and Vegetation Changes for Species

Among the species of management concern within the Fort Hood study area is the black-capped vireo (*Vireo atricapilla*). The black-capped vireo is a federally listed endangered species that breeds at Fort Hood from approximately March to August (Tazik and others, 1993a). The shrubby, short, woody vegetation used by black-capped vireos for nesting often is early seral vegetation that, if left undisturbed, will transition into mature forest and woodland. Thus, both natural and anthropogenic disturbance regimes are important for maintaining black-capped vireo habitat across the Fort Hood study area (Bailey and Thompson, 2007; Grzybowski and others, 1994). The projected future vegetation simulated for the Fort Hood study area indicates that broadleaved summergreen PFTs will continue to be a component of the vegetation. Maintaining this vegetation in the preferred seral stage for the black-capped vireo will require relatively frequent disturbance events, such as fires (both prescribed and natural) or vegetation disturbance produced

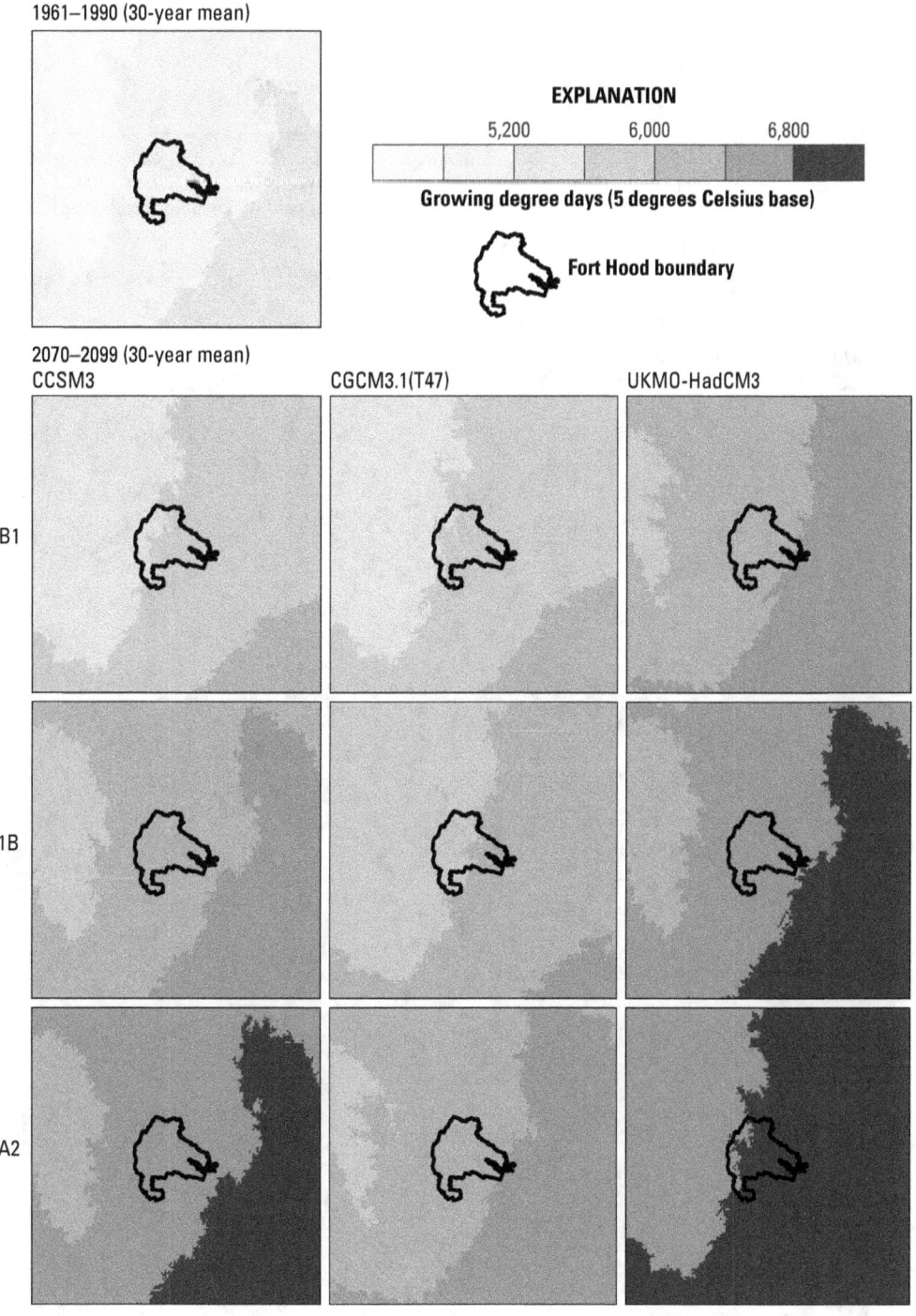

Figure 12. Mean annual growing degree days (on a 5 degrees Celsius base) for the Fort Hood study area and the boundary of Fort Hood (black line). Top row: 1961–1990 (30-year mean) mean annual growing degree days (on a 5 degrees Celsius base) calculated from downscaled CRU CL 2.0 (New and others, 2002) and CRU TS 2.1 (Mitchell and Jones, 2005) data. Bottom rows: 2070–2099 (30-year mean) mean annual growing degree days (on a 5 degrees Celsius base) calculated from downscaled CCSM3 (Collins and others, 2006a), CGCM3.1(T47) (Scinocca and others, 2008), and UKMO-HadCM3 (Pope and others, 2000) simulations produced using the B1, A1B, and A2 greenhouse gas emissions scenarios.

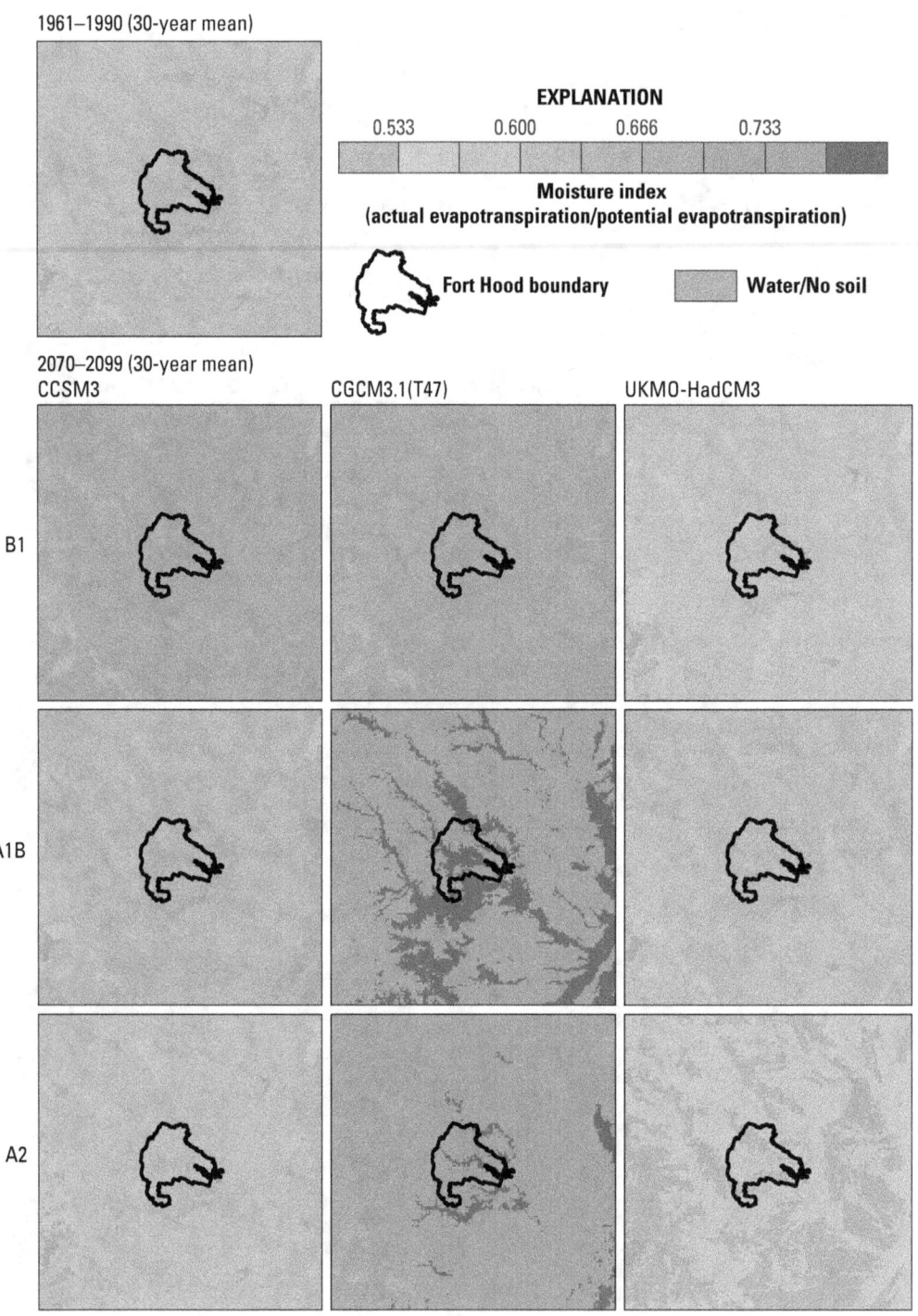

Figure 13.   Mean annual moisture index (actual evapotranspiration divided by potential evapotranspiration) for the Fort Hood study area and the boundary of Fort Hood (black line). Top row: 1961–1990 (30-year mean) mean annual moisture index calculated from downscaled CRU CL 2.0 (New and others, 2002) and CRU TS 2.1 (Mitchell and Jones, 2005) data. Bottom rows: 2070–2099 (30-year mean) mean annual moisture index calculated from downscaled CCSM3 (Collins and others, 2006a), CGCM3.1(T47) (Scinocca and others, 2008), and UKMO-HadCM3 (Pope and others, 2000) simulations produced using the B1, A1B, and A2 greenhouse gas emissions scenarios.

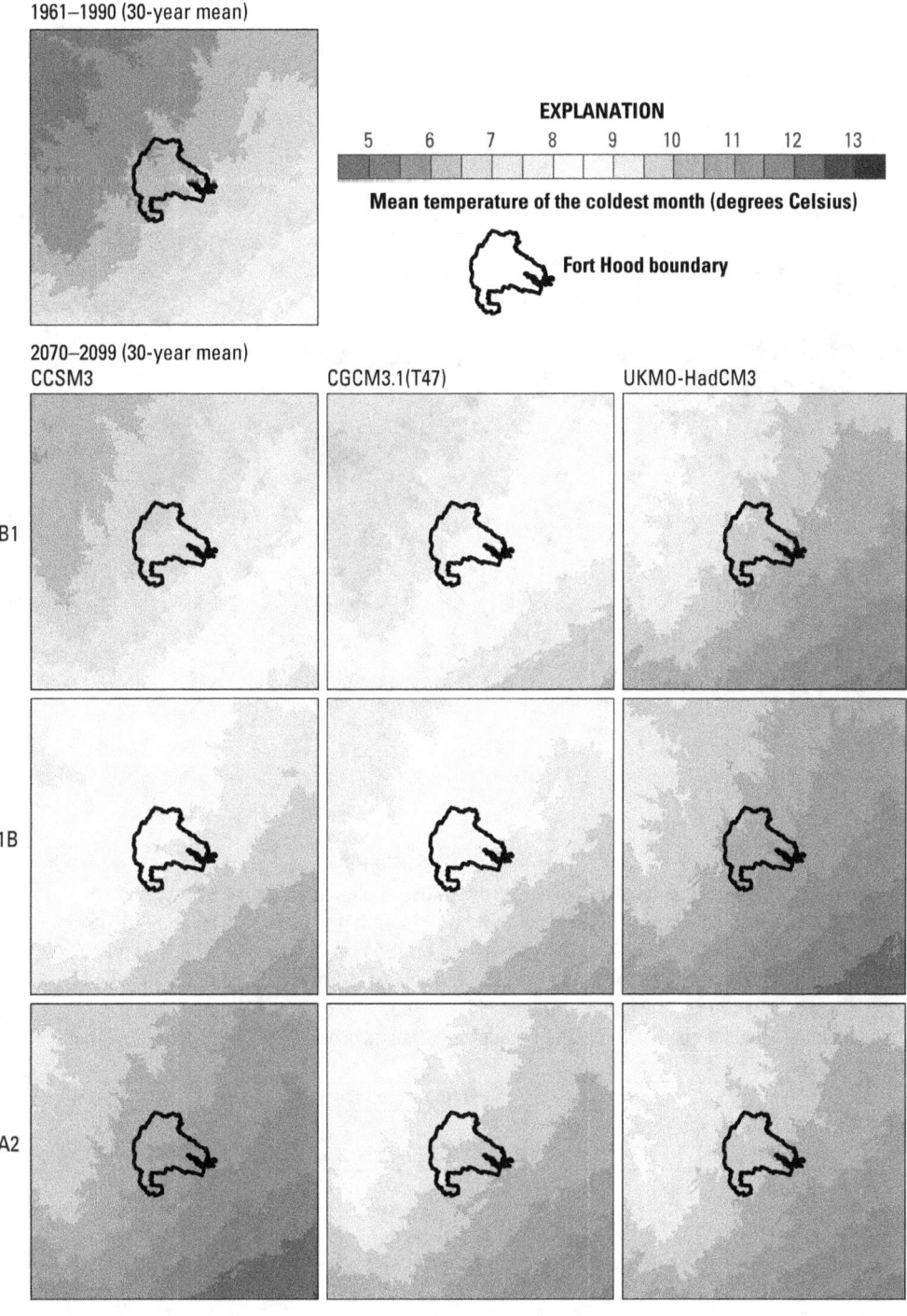

Figure 14.   Mean temperature of the coldest month (degrees Celsius) for the Fort Hood study area and the boundary of Fort Hood (black line). Top row: 1961–1990 (30-year mean) mean temperature of the coldest month calculated from downscaled CRU CL 2.0 (New and others, 2002) and CRU TS 2.1 (Mitchell and Jones, 2005) data. Bottom rows: 2070–2099 (30-year mean) mean temperature of the coldest month calculated from downscaled CCSM3 (Collins and others, 2006a), CGCM3.1(T47) (Scinocca and others, 2008), and UKMO-HadCM3 (Pope and others, 2000) simulations produced using the B1, A1B, and A2 greenhouse gas emissions scenarios.

Figure 15. High quality black-capped vireo *(Vireo atricapilla)* habitat at Fort Hood Military Reservation, Texas. This site is located in an intensive study area used for annual monitoring of vireo productivity. The site originally was cleared by bulldozer and then abandoned in approximately 1980. Limited management has occurred at the site since the original disturbance. The dominant shrub species in the image is shin oak *(Quercus sinuata* var. *breviloba)*, a preferred nesting substrate for the vireo. Sparse Ashe juniper *(Juniperus ashei)* is also present (Photograph taken by C.B. Wilsey, 2007).

Table 7. Mean foliar projective cover (percent) for needleleaved, broadleaved, and grass plant functional types (PFTs) simulated by LPJ (Sitch and others, 2003) for 1961–1990 (30-year mean) and for 2070–2099 (30-year mean) for the Fort Hood study area. LPJ was run using climate data from downscaled CCSM3 (Collins and others, 2006a), CGCM3.1(T47) (Scinocca and others, 2008), and UKMO-HadCM3 (Pope and others, 2000) coupled atmosphere-ocean general circulation model simulations produced using the B1, A1B, and A2 greenhouse gas emissions scenarios.

Plant functional type	Foliar projective cover (percent)			
	Historical (1961–1990)	B1 (2070–2099)	A1B (2070–2099)	A2 (2070–2099)
Needleleaved	13.26			
CCSM3	--	16.94	13.42	11.26
CGCM3.1(T47)	--	27.00	19.43	25.57
UKMO-HadCM3	--	10.76	4.84	11.20
Broadleaved	43.77			
CCSM3	--	38.06	48.10	34.21
CGCM3.1(T47)	--	62.62	70.01	66.41
UKMO-HadCM3	--	23.45	51.70	27.25
Grass	40.99			
CCSM3	--	43.99	37.56	52.74
CGCM3.1(T47)	--	9.18	9.84	7.16
UKMO-HadCM3	--	63.83	40.15	58.79

Table 8. Mean foliar projective cover (percent) of needleleaved evergreen plant functional type (PFT) individuals less than 20 years old for the Fort Hood study area (2070–2099 30-year mean) as simulated by LPJ-GUESS (Smith and others, 2001) with fires suppressed ("no fire") and with fires simulated ("fire"). LPJ-GUESS was run using climate data from downscaled CCSM3 (Collins and others, 2006a), CGCM3.1(T47) (Scinocca and others, 2008), and UKMO-HadCM3 (Pope and others, 2000) coupled atmosphere-ocean general circulation model (AOGCM) simulations produced using the B1, A1B, and A2 greenhouse gas emissions scenarios. Values listed under each emissions scenario are mean values from the three AOGCMs.

LPJ-GUESS simulation	Foliar projective cover (percent)		
	B1	A1B	A2
Broadleaved PFTs less than 20 years old			
No fire	3.93	3.90	3.89
Fire	1.55	1.55	1.55

by military activities (Tazik and others, 1993b; Guretzky and others, 2006). For example, Tazik and others (1993a) reported black-capped vireo habitat produced in an area where the vegetation had been disturbed by a bulldozer.

Another species of management concern in the Fort Hood study area is the golden-cheeked warbler, which also is a federally listed endangered species (U.S. Fish and Wildlife Service, 1990a). The warbler is a Neotropical migrant that breeds in central Texas and spends the winter in Mexico and Central America (Anders and Dearborn, 2004). It nests in closed canopy juniper-oak vegetation patches that contain numerous small trees, especially junipers, and that also have juniper cover consisting of trees greater than 2 m high (Dearborn and Sanchez, 2001). Reidy and others (2009) propose managing for patches of mature juniper-oak vegetation larger than 100 ha to increase golden-cheeked warbler nesting success.

As described above, the golden-cheeked warbler generally requires vegetation greater than 2 m high for nesting, while the black-capped vireo generally requires vegetation less than 2 m high for nesting. These different habitat requirements present challenges for managing vegetation under climate change to maintain both low stature, early seral vegetation for black-capped vireos and large patches of taller, more mature vegetation for golden-cheeked warblers. The simulated vegetation indicates that the broadleaved and needleleaved PFTs that provide nesting habitat in the study area today would continue to be present under future climate conditions. For both the black-capped vireo and golden-cheeked warbler, continued habitat loss and fragmentation also are considered significant threats to the species' survival (Hayden and others, 2001).

The Fort Hood study area supports other species of management concern. Whooping cranes may periodically use habitat in the study area during migration between southern Texas wintering grounds and breeding sites in Canada (Hayden and others, 2001). Similar to wood storks, whooping crane reproductive success is affected by prey availability near nesting sites, which is linked to water levels (Spalding and others, 2009). The study area also includes endemic cave fauna (Hayden and others, 2001).

Fort Irwin Study Area

Site Description

The Fort Irwin study area (28,440 km²) is located in the Mojave Desert. Estimated elevations of the study area grid points range from approximately -7 m to approximately 2,381 m above sea level (fig. 3; Gesch and others, 2002). The study area spans three different ecoregions as defined by Bailey (1997): (1) deserts on sand, (2) mixed forest-coniferous forest-alpine meadow, and (3) Mediterranean woodland or shrub-mixed or coniferous forest-steppe or meadow. Fort Irwin lies almost entirely within the deserts on sand ecoregion. The Fort Irwin study area encompasses six different potential natural vegetation categories as defined by Küchler (1993): (1) creosote bush, (2) saltbush-greasewood, (3) juniper-pinyon woodland, (4) Great Basin sagebrush, (5) chaparral, and (6) mixed conifers. Almost all of Fort Irwin lies within the creosote bush potential natural vegetation region (Küchler, 1993, fig. 16). Dominant plant species across the study area include creosote bush (*Larrea tridentata*) and white bursage (*Ambrosia dumosa*). Studies that describe the vegetation at Fort Irwin include Brandt and others (1997) and Berry and others (2006).

Climate

The estimated 1961–1990 30-year mean temperatures for the Fort Irwin study area are 17.8 °C annually, 16.3 °C in spring (March–May), 28.5 °C in summer (June–August),

Figure 16. Open rangeland at Fort Irwin, California. These lower elevation lands with sparse shrub cover serve as habitat for the desert tortoise on the installation (Photograph taken by B.A. Bancroft, 2007).

18.4 °C in fall (September–November), and 8.0 °C in winter (December–February). The estimated 1961–1990 30-year mean total precipitation for the study area is 129 mm annually, 29 mm in spring (March–May), 18 mm in summer (June–August), 26 mm in fall (September–November), and 56 mm in winter (December–February). The 1961–1990 30-year mean bioclimatic values estimated for the study area are 4,697 GDD5, 0.0815 for the moisture index (AET/PET), and 6.28 °C for the mean temperature of the coldest month.

Projected future mean annual temperature changes for the region for 2070–2099 (30-year mean) varied from an increase of 2.19 °C simulated by CCSM3 under the B1 emissions scenario to an increase of 4.74 °C simulated by both CCSM3 and UKMO-HadCM3 under the A2 emissions scenario (table 9, fig. 17). Seasonal mean temperature changes varied from an increase of 1.76 °C for winter (December–February) simulated by CCSM3 under the B1 emissions scenario to an increase of 6.04 °C for summer (June–August) simulated by UKMO-HadCM3 under the A2 emissions scenario (table 9). Projected future mean annual precipitation changes for the region for 2070–2099 (30-year mean) varied from a decrease of 21 percent simulated by CGCM3.1(T47) under the A2 emissions scenario to an increase of 56 percent simulated by CCSM3 under the A2 emissions scenario (table 9, fig. 18). Projected seasonal mean precipitation changes varied from a decrease of 38 percent simulated by CGCM3.1(T47) and UKMO-HadCM3 under the A2 emissions scenario for March-May to an increase of 477 percent simulated by CCSM3 under the A2 emissions scenario for June–August (table 9).

The projected future precipitation anomalies are calculated as percent change relative to the 1961–1990 30-year mean base period values. In some cases the projected changes are quite large but these large percent changes reflect, in part, that precipitation amounts at Fort Irwin are relatively small. For example, the estimated 1961–1990 (30-year mean) summer precipitation for the study area is 18 mm. A 10 percent increase in summer precipitation would represent only a 1.8 mm increase in the total amount of summer precipitation. Thus, relatively large projected percent changes in precipitation may reflect relatively small amounts of water.

GDD5 values were projected to increase under all nine AOGCM and emissions scenario combinations (table 10, fig. 19). The moisture index (AET/PET) was projected to decrease from 0.0815 (1961–1990 30-year mean) to 0.0758 (2070–2099 30-year mean) under the CGCM3.1(T47) A2 simulations but to increase under the other eight AOGCM and emissions scenario combinations (table 10, fig. 20). Increases in the moisture index may result from increases in AET, decreases in PET, or a combination of changes in both AET and PET. An increase in the moisture index generally indicates that more moisture is available for vegetation. Mean temperature of the coldest month increased under all nine scenarios (table 10, fig. 21) with projected mean temperatures of the coldest month ranging from 7.71 °C simulated by CCSM3 under the B1 emissions scenario to 10.05 °C simulated by CGCM3.1(T47) under the A2 emissions scenario for 2070–2099 (30-year mean).

Table 9.   Mean annual and seasonal temperature (degrees Celsius) and precipitation (percent) anomalies for 2070–2099 (30-year mean) for the Fort Irwin study area. Anomalies were calculated from downscaled CCSM3 (Collins and others, 2006a), CGCM3.1(T47) (Scinocca and others, 2008), and UKMO-HadCM3 (Pope and others, 2000) coupled atmosphere-ocean general circulation model simulations produced using the B1, A1B, and A2 greenhouse gas emissions scenarios.

| Model simulation | Greenhouse gas emissions scenario | | | | | |
| | B1 | | A1B | | A2 | |
	Temperature[1] (degrees Celsius)	Precipitation[2] (percent)	Temperature[1] (degrees Celsius)	Precipitation[2] (percent)	Temperature[1] (degrees Celsius)	Precipitation[2] (percent)
Annual						
CCSM3	+2.19	+16	+3.60	-7	+4.74	+56
CGCM3.1(T47)	+2.37	-4	+3.05	-2	+4.21	-21
UKMO-HadCM3	+3.31	-8	+4.32	-1	+4.74	+39
December–February						
CCSM3	+1.76	-11	+3.22	-7	+4.12	-11
CGCM3.1(T47)	+2.14	+0	+2.58	-5	+3.74	-14
UKMO-HadCM3	+2.49	-25	+3.37	-20	+3.55	-12
March–May						
CCSM3	+1.82	-11	+3.59	-31	+4.42	-34
CGCM3.1(T47)	+2.70	-18	+2.76	-11	+4.25	-38
UKMO-HadCM3	+2.93	-31	+3.72	-17	+4.34	-38
June–August						
CCSM3	+2.47	+183	+3.88	+56	+5.53	+477
CGCM3.1(T47)	+2.78	+11	+3.69	+17	+4.78	-17
UKMO-HadCM3	+4.23	+61	+5.55	+56	+6.04	+122
September–November						
CCSM3	+2.70	-15	+3.71	-23	+4.98	+4
CGCM3.1(T47)	+1.87	+4	+3.16	+0	+4.04	-19
UKMO-HadCM3	+3.57	+8	+4.64	+15	+5.05	+177
September–March						
CCSM3	+2.21	-7	+3.61	-17	+4.55	-12
CGCM3.1(T47)	+2.12	+0	+2.90	+2	+4.00	-17
UKMO-HadCM3	+3.02	-14	+3.91	-4	+4.18	+39

[1]Temperature anomalies were calculated as 2070–2099 (30-year mean) simulated temperature minus 1961–1990 (30-year mean) simulated temperature.

[2]Precipitation anomalies were calculated by multiplying by 100 the quotient of 2070–2099 (30-year mean) simulated precipitation divided by 1961–1990 (30-year mean) simulated precipitation.

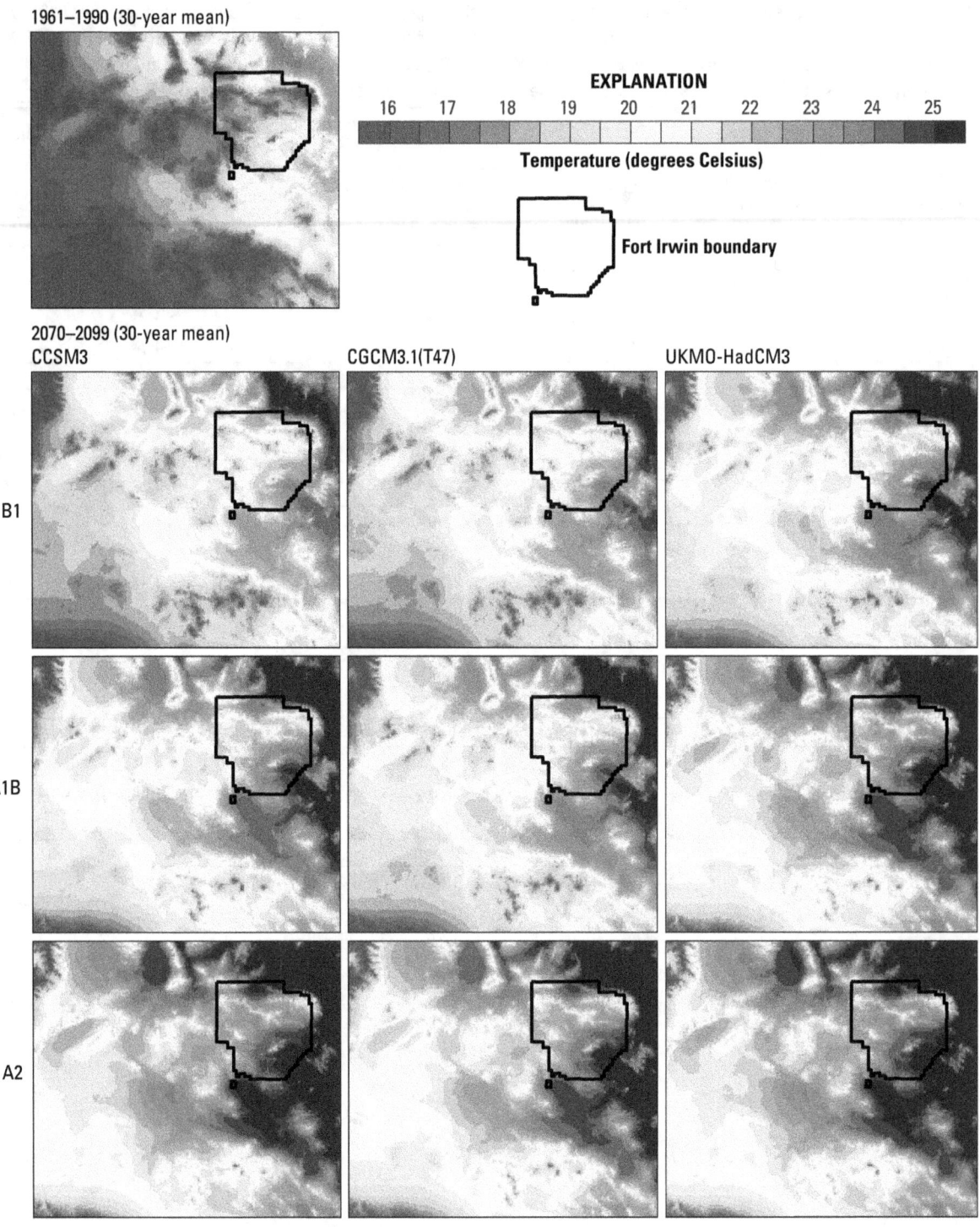

Figure 17. Mean annual temperature (degrees Celsius) for the Fort Irwin study area and the boundary of Fort Irwin (black line). Top row: 1961–1990 (30-year mean) mean annual temperature calculated from downscaled CRU CL 2.0 (New and others, 2002) and CRU TS 2.1 (Mitchell and Jones, 2005) data. Bottom rows: 2070–2099 (30-year mean) mean annual temperature calculated from downscaled CCSM3 (Collins and others, 2006a), CGCM3.1(T47) (Scinocca and others, 2008), and UKMO-HadCM3 (Pope and others, 2000) simulations produced using the B1, A1B, and A2 greenhouse gas emissions scenarios.

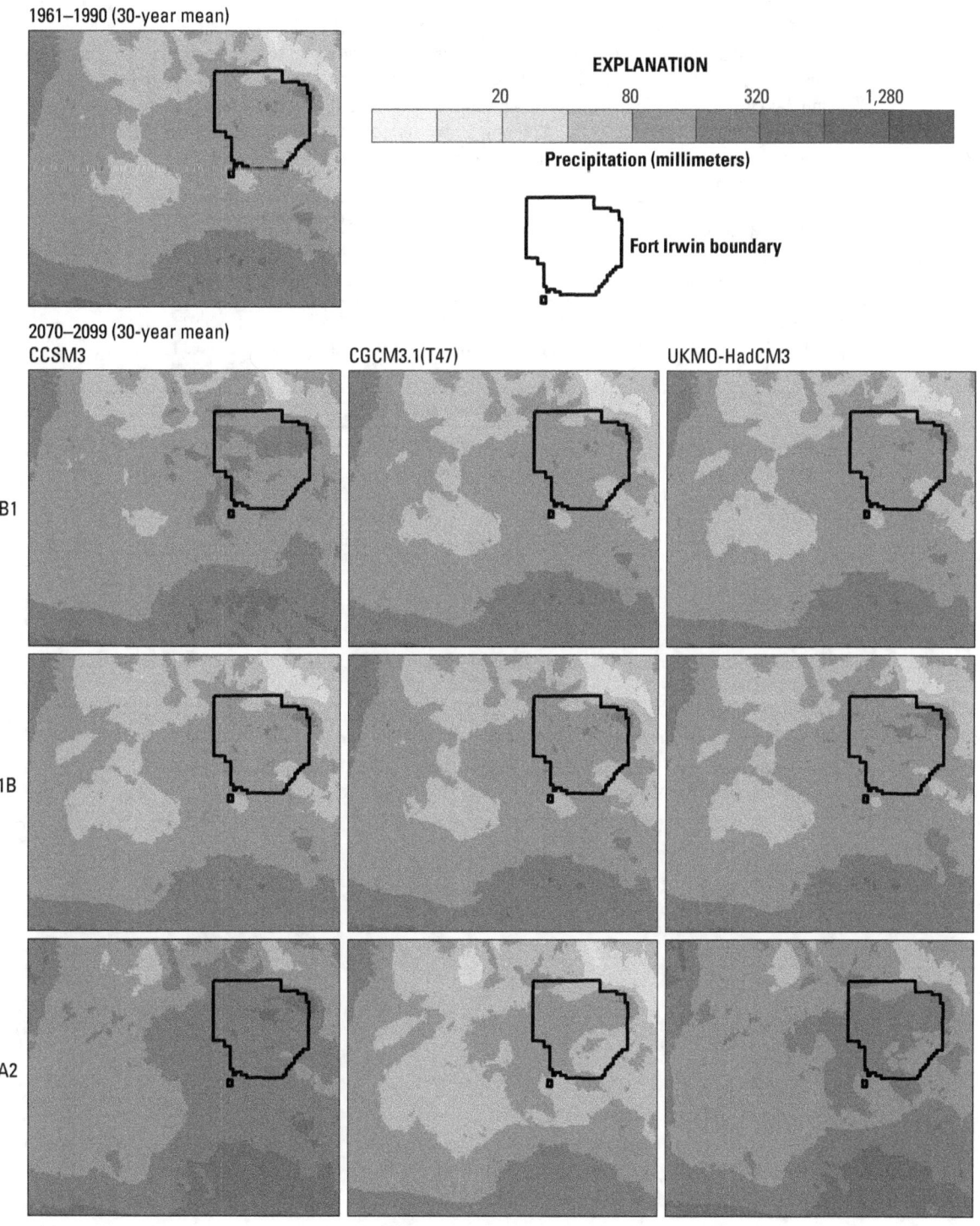

Figure 18. Mean total annual precipitation (millimeters) for the Fort Irwin study area and the boundary of Fort Irwin (black line). Top row: 1961–1990 (30-year mean) mean total annual precipitation calculated from downscaled CRU CL 2.0 (New and others, 2002) and CRU TS 2.1 (Mitchell and Jones, 2005) data. Bottom rows: 2070–2099 (30-year mean) mean total annual precipitation calculated from downscaled CCSM3 (Collins and others, 2006a), CGCM3.1(T47) (Scinocca and others, 2008), and UKMO-HadCM3 (Pope and others, 2000) simulations produced using the B1, A1B, and A2 greenhouse gas emissions scenarios.

Table 10. Mean annual growing degree days on a 5 degrees Celsius base (GDD5) anomalies, mean annual moisture index, and mean temperature of the coldest month anomalies for 2070–2099 (30-year mean) for the Fort Irwin study area. Values calculated using data downscaled from CCSM3 (Collins and others, 2006a), CGCM3.1(T47) (Scinocca and others, 2008), and UKMO-HadCM3 (Pope and others, 2000) coupled atmosphere-ocean general circulation model simulations produced using the B1, A1B, and A2 greenhouse gas emissions scenarios.

Model simulation	Greenhouse gas emissions scenario		
	B1	A1B	A2
Mean annual growing degree days on a 5 degrees Celsius base anomalies (percent)[1]			
CCSM3	+17	+28	+37
CGCM3.1(T47)	+18	+24	+33
UKMO-HadCM3	+26	+34	+37
Mean annual moisture index (AET/PET)[2]			
CCSM3	0.1007	0.0823	0.1216
CGCM3.1(T47)	0.0915	0.0955	0.0758
UKMO-HadCM3	0.0848	0.0953	0.1191
Mean temperature of the coldest month anomalies (degrees Celsius)[3]			
CCSM3	+1.43	+2.67	+3.40
CGCM3.1(T47)	+2.03	+2.31	+3.77
UKMO-HadCM3	+2.81	+3.40	+3.17

[1]Growing degree day anomalies calculated by multiplying by 100 the quotient of 2070–2099 (30-year mean) GDD5 divided by 1961–1990 (30-year mean) GDD5.

[2]Moisture index calculated as actual evapotranspiration divided by potential evapotranspiration. Note that moisture index values are simulated 2070–2099 30-year mean values and not anomalies for 2070–2099.

[3]Mean temperature of the coldest month anomalies calculated as 2070–2099 (30-year mean) values minus 1961–1990 (30-year) mean values.

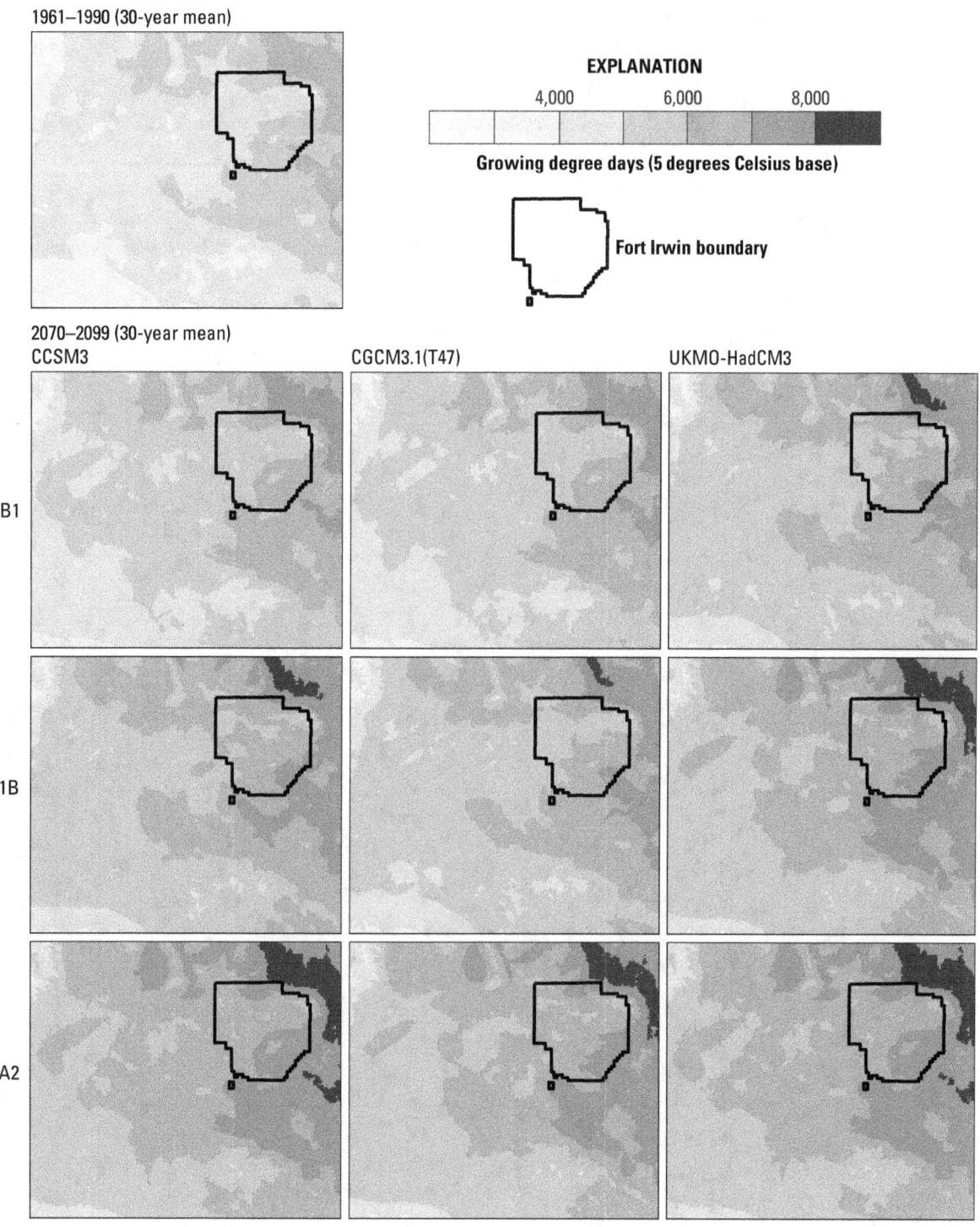

Figure 19. Mean annual growing degree days (on a 5 degrees Celsius base) for the Fort Irwin study area and the boundary of Fort Irwin (black line). Top row: 1961–1990 (30-year mean) mean annual growing degree days (on a 5 degrees Celsius base) calculated from downscaled CRU CL 2.0 (New and others, 2002) and CRU TS 2.1 (Mitchell and Jones, 2005) data. Bottom rows: 2070–2099 (30-year mean) mean annual growing degree days (on a 5 degrees Celsius base) calculated from downscaled CCSM3 (Collins and others, 2006a), CGCM3.1(T47) (Scinocca and others, 2008), and UKMO-HadCM3 (Pope and others, 2000) simulations produced using the B1, A1B, and A2 greenhouse gas emissions scenarios.

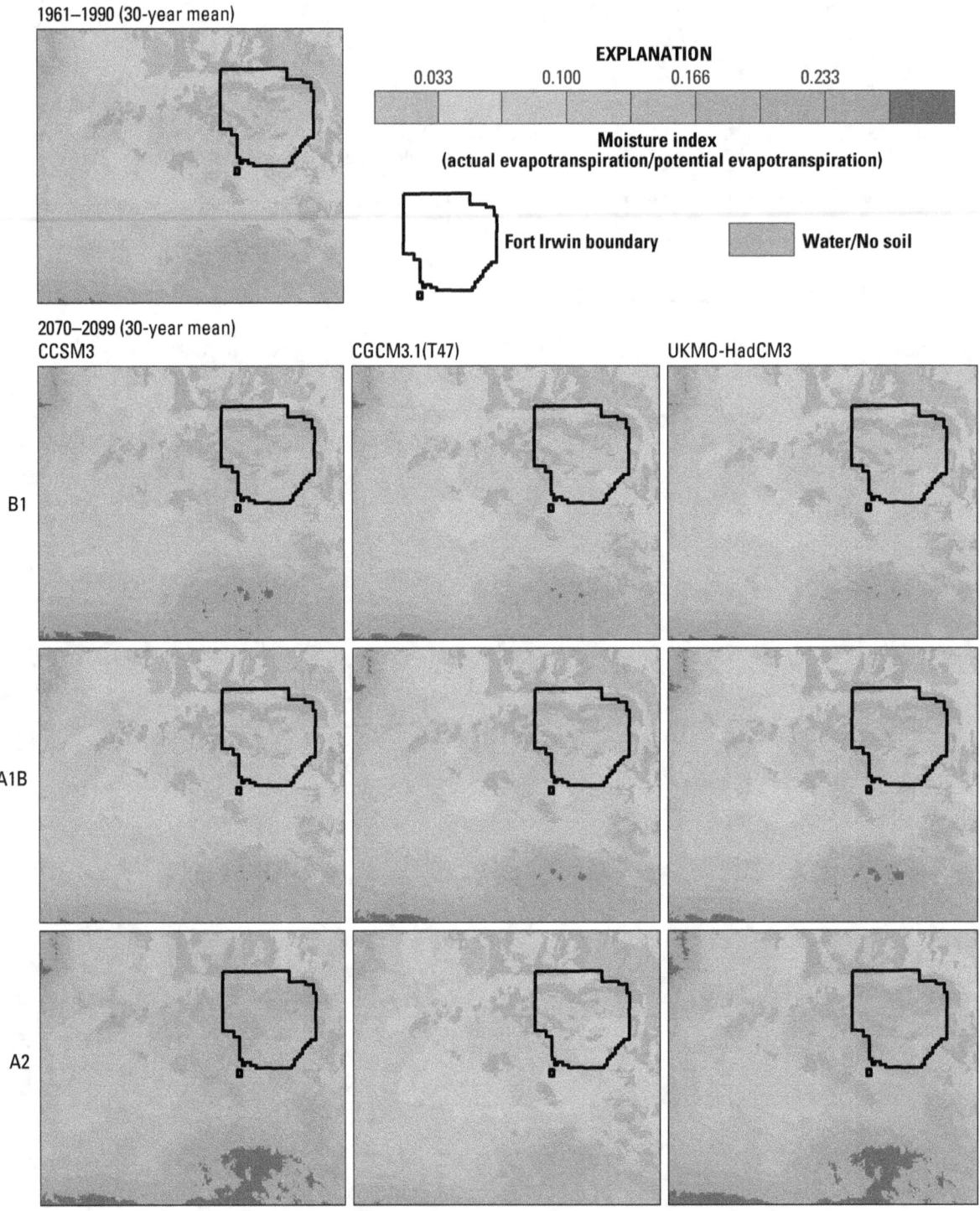

Figure 20.   Mean annual moisture index (actual evapotranspiration divided by potential evapotranspiration) for the Fort Irwin study area and the boundary of Fort Irwin (black line). Top row: 1961–1990 (30-year mean) mean annual moisture index calculated from downscaled CRU CL 2.0 (New and others, 2002) and CRU TS 2.1 (Mitchell and Jones, 2005) data. Bottom rows: 2070–2099 (30-year mean) mean annual moisture index calculated from downscaled CCSM3 (Collins and others, 2006a), CGCM3.1(T47) (Scinocca and others, 2008), and UKMO-HadCM3 (Pope and others, 2000) simulations produced using the B1, A1B, and A2 greenhouse gas emissions scenarios.

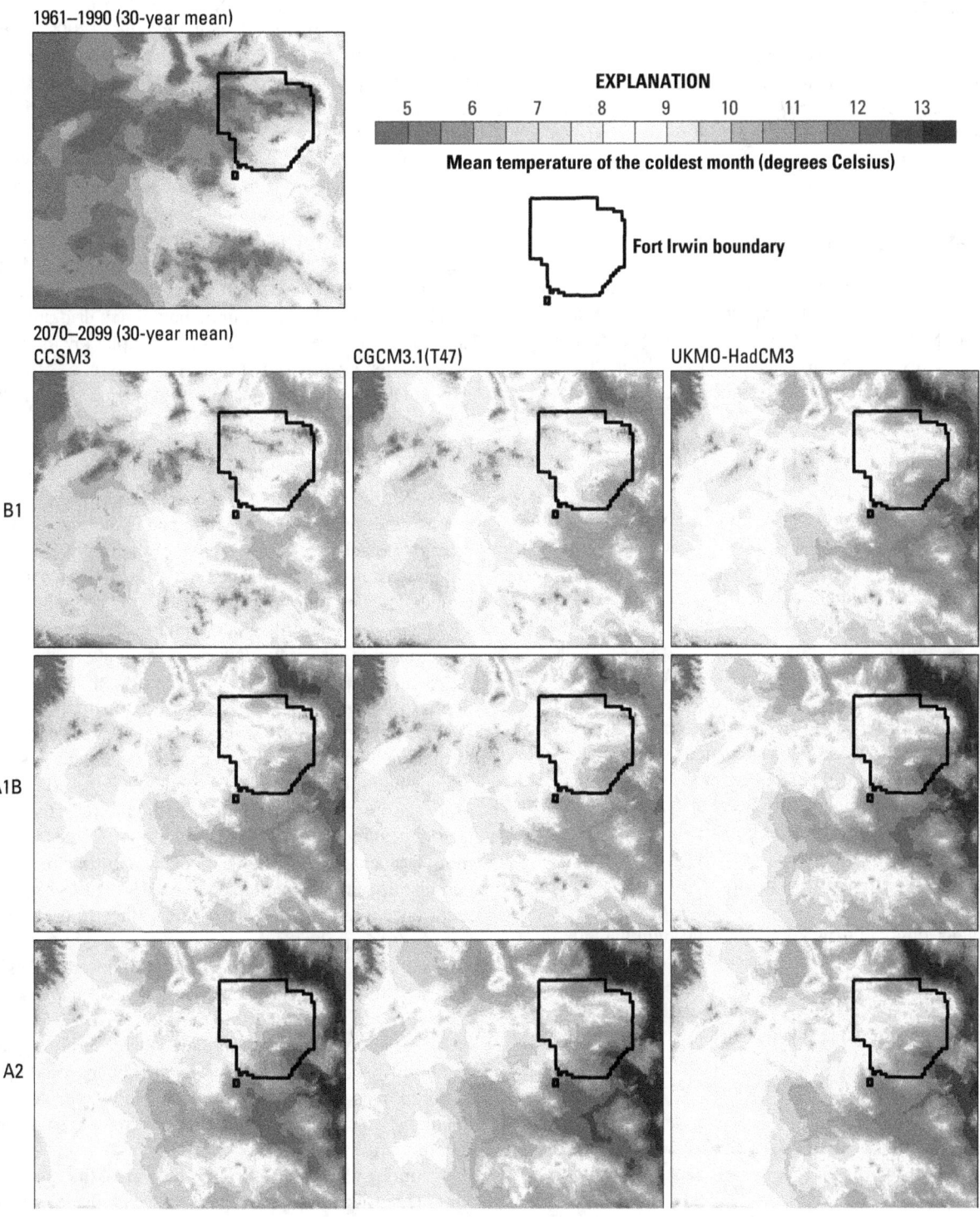

Figure 21. Mean temperature of the coldest month (degrees Celsius) for the Fort Irwin study area and the boundary of Fort Irwin (black line). Top row: 1961–1990 (30-year mean) mean temperature of the coldest month calculated from downscaled CRU CL 2.0 (New and others, 2002) and CRU TS 2.1 (Mitchell and Jones, 2005) data. Bottom rows: 2070–2099 (30-year mean) mean temperature of the coldest month calculated from downscaled CCSM3 (Collins and others, 2006a), CGCM3.1(T47) (Scinocca and others, 2008), and UKMO-HadCM3 (Pope and others, 2000) simulations produced using the B1, A1B, and A2 greenhouse gas emissions scenarios.

Vegetation

Vegetation for the Fort Irwin study area was simulated using LPJ. Particular attention was paid to evaluating projected changes in the grass PFT. This PFT best represents the grass and forb taxa that are the main food source of the desert tortoise (*Gopherus agassizii*), which is a species of management concern in the region (Krzysik, 1994).

Vegetation Model Parameters

For the LPJ vegetation simulations for the Fort Irwin study area we used the PFT parameters described in tables 1 and 2 of Sitch and others (2003) except for fire resistance values. Fire resistance values were set to 0.12 for all woody PFTs based on general fire sensitivities of desert plants (Brooks and Matchett, 2006).

Simulated Historical Vegetation

LPJ simulated a mix of four PFTs across the Fort Irwin study area under 1961–1990 (30-year mean) climate conditions: needleleaved evergreen, broadleaved evergreen, and broadleaved deciduous woody PFTs, and the C3 grass PFT. These PFTs match those represented by the potential natural vegetation defined by Küchler (1993) for the study area. LPJ simulated a total percent vegetation cover of 23 percent (1961–1990 30-year mean) for all simulated PFTs across the Fort Irwin study area with the remaining area simulated as bare ground. This simulated percent cover value falls within the observed percent cover values of 4–28 percent for perennial plants reported by Berry and others (2006) from 21 vegetation plots measured at Fort Irwin.

Simulated Future Vegetation

Under future climate conditions, the combination of PFTs simulated for the Fort Irwin study area do not change. Projected percent cover for the grass PFT is projected to increase under all nine AOGCM and emissions scenario combinations (table 11). This increase in grass cover could represent future increases of both native and nonnative species (Brooks and Esque, 2002).

Implications of Future Climate and Vegetation Changes for Species

The desert tortoise (*Gopherus agassizii*) is a federally listed threatened species (U.S. Fish and Wildlife Service, 1990b) that occurs in desert regions in the southwestern part of the United States, in northwestern Mexico, and within the boundaries of Fort Irwin (Berry and others, 2006). Desert tortoises are well adapted to arid environments where water resources are both scarce and variable. They may be able to go for a year or longer without drinking water (Peterson, 1996) and they obtain moisture from the forbs and grasses that make up their main food sources, including both exotic and native forbs and grasses (Hazard and others, 2009). Hereford and others (2006) and Henen and others (1998) discuss precipitation variability over the Mojave Desert and the importance of winter precipitation for determining the amount of spring grasses.

For this study we used monthly precipitation totals from AOGCM simulations of future climate change. These monthly totals do not provide information on potential future changes in the frequency and intensity of precipitation events, which will affect the productivity of the vegetation that makes up the tortoises' diet (Beatley, 1969). Precipitation variability also will be important in determining how much drinking water is available to desert tortoises. For example, low intensity precipitation events consisting of small volumes of water may quickly evaporate whereas more intense precipitation events may allow water to pool for short periods of time, providing a source of drinking water for the tortoises (Medica and others, 1980). Precipitation still is difficult for many AOGCMs to simulate and the future climate projections we examined differed in the direction and magnitude of projected precipitation changes (table 9). All of the future climate projections, however, indicated potential increases in winter temperatures ranging from 1.76 °C to 4.12 °C (table 9) and LPJ-GUESS projected an increase in the amount of grass PFT cover under all of the future climate simulations, which could represent increased amounts of spring forage available to the desert tortoises when they emerge from hibernation.

Desert tortoises are susceptible to a variety of disturbance events, including anthropogenic disturbances such as cattle grazing and military training activities (Krzysik, 1994). Under projected future climate conditions, the fire recurrence interval is projected to decrease (that is, fires are projected to become more frequent) under all nine model and emissions scenario combinations from a simulated 1961–1990 (30-year mean) fire recurrence interval of 24 years. Under three future simulations (table 11) the projected fire recurrence interval for 2070–2099 (30-year mean) is 13 years. Fires can kill desert tortoises and increased future fire occurrence could lead to increased desert tortoise mortality (Esque and others 2003). These projected increases in fire frequency simulated under future climate conditions would be in addition to already observed increases in fire frequencies that have occurred with the invasion of nonnative and invasive plant species across the study area (Brooks and Esque, 2002).

Among plant species in the study area, the Lane Mountain milk vetch (*Astragalus jaegerianus*) is a cryptic perennial plant that sprouts annually from a persistent taproot (U.S. Fish and Wildlife Service, 2008). It occurs in a limited area of the Mojave Desert and is a federally listed endangered species that was recently recommended for downlisting to threatened status (U.S. Fish and Wildlife Service, 2008). Lane Mountain milk vetch grows in close association with desert shrubs, particularly Nevada jointfir (*Ephedra nevadensis*) and Cooper goldenbush (*Ericameria cooperi*), although it also is found growing alone (Brandt and others, 1997). Both field

Table 11. Mean annual grass cover anomalies (percent) and fire return intervals (years) for 2070–2099 (30-year mean) as simulated by LPJ (Sitch and others, 2003) for the Fort Irwin study area.

Model simulation	Greenhouse gas emissions scenario		
	B1	A1B	A2
Grass cover anomalies (percent)[1]			
CCSM3	+61	+23	+68
CGCM3.1(T47)	+38	+44	+15
UKMO-HadCM3	+2	+35	+67
Fire return interval (years)			
CCSM3	15	15	13
CGCM3.1(T47)	16	13	16
UKMO-HadCM3	19	19	13

[1]Grass cover anomalies were calculated by multiplying by 100 the quotient of 2070–2099 (30-year mean) grass cover values divided by 1961–1990 (30-year mean) grass cover values.

and greenhouse studies indicate that the timing and amount of precipitation during the year is important for allowing individuals to survive periods of drought. Rundel and others (2007) proposed that significant population recruitment for the Lane Mountain milk vetch may occur only in years with large amounts of precipitation. Both fire and predation also are considered to have significant effects on Lane Mountain milk vetch populations (Rundel and others, 2007).

Conclusions

Annual and seasonal mean temperatures are projected to increase in the future for the Fort Benning, Fort Hood, and Fort Irwin study areas under all nine AOGCM and greenhouse gas emissions scenario combinations. This agreement is similar to that reported in the Intergovernmental Panel on Climate Change (IPCC) Fourth Assessment Report (Meehl and others, 2007b), which found that all of the AOGCM simulations that were assessed for nonmitigated greenhouse gas emissions scenarios projected increases in global mean annual surface air temperatures. Annual and seasonal total precipitation amounts projected for the three study areas display less agreement. Frequently, under the same emission scenario, one AOGCM will simulate increased precipitation while another AOGCM will simulate decreased precipitation. Future precipitation changes will be important for maintaining both terrestrial and aquatic species' habitats at all three study sites, but the uncertainties associated with AOGCM precipitation simulations limit the conclusions that can be drawn at this time about future precipitation changes and their potential effects.

For each of the study areas, the vegetation projected for the future is relatively similar to the vegetation simulated

under historical climate conditions. In general, the same combinations of PFTs are simulated to persist at each site in the future, although some PFTs are projected to increase in coverage while other PFTs are projected to decrease in coverage. That a PFT is simulated to persist at a site does not necessarily mean that the mix of species will remain the same in the future since a single PFT may represent multiple plant species. The vegetation simulations also indicate that changes in the magnitude and frequency of future fire occurrence will have a significant effect on vegetation. Other disturbance regimes, such as disease and pest outbreaks, also may be important in determining the future distribution of vegetation but were not simulated as part of this study.

The future climate and vegetation changes projected for the study areas would affect plant and animal species in a variety of ways. Some species may be affected directly by future changes in temperature and precipitation. In other cases, projected climate changes may indirectly affect species by altering disturbance regimes that maintain important habitat or by affecting the timing and availability of food resources. In this study, we focused on the potential effects of projected climate and vegetation changes for species that are of management concern within the study areas. As climate changes, species that currently are not considered of management concern may require increasing management attention. The species composition of the study areas also may change as species' ranges expand or contract in response to climate changes (Parmesan, 2006). Future changes in species composition, including the presence of nonnative invasive species, could have significant consequences ranging from altering competitive interactions among species to affecting disturbance regimes (Walther and others, 2002).

Climate change is only one of many factors affecting the viability of species and habitat. Land-use changes resulting in the fragmentation, disturbance, and loss of habitat may be more important in the near term than climate changes for determining the survival of species (Sala and others, 2000). For example, some of the bird species discussed in this report are Neotropical migrants, such as golden-cheeked warblers, that may be present in the study areas only during the breeding season (Anders and Dearborn, 2004). For these species, land use and climate change effects on their wintering habitat also will affect their populations.

Acknowledgments

We thank Steve Hostetler and Allen Solomon for their review of earlier drafts of this document, J. Neufeldt and M. Thornton for discussions about individual species, and Richard Pelltier for assistance in developing the study grids and figures. Funding for this report was provided by the U.S. Department of Defense Strategic Environmental Research and Development Program (SERDP) grant SI-1541. S. L. Shafer was funded by the U.S. Geological Survey Climate and Land Use Change Research and Development Program. We also acknowledge the modeling groups, the Program for Climate Model Diagnosis and Intercomparison (PCMDI) and the WCRP's Working Group on Coupled Modelling (WGCM) for their roles in making available the WCRP CMIP3 multi-model dataset. Support of this dataset is provided by the Office of Science, U.S. Department of Energy.

References Cited

Anders, A.D., and Dearborn, D.C., 2004, Population trends of the endangered golden-cheeked warbler at Fort Hood, Texas, from 1992–2001: The Southwestern Naturalist, v. 49, p. 39–47.

Bachelet, D., Lenihan, J., Drapek, R., and Neilson, R., 2008, VEMAP vs VINCERA: A DGVM sensitivity to differences in climate scenarios: Global and Planetary Change, v. 64, p. 38–48.

Bader, D.C., Covey, C., Gutowski, W.J., Jr., Held, I.M., Kunkel, K.E., Miller, R.L., Tokmakian, R.T., and Zhang, M.H., 2008, Climate models: An assessment of strengths and limitations. A report by the U.S. Climate Change Science Program and the Subcommittee on Global Change Research: Washington, D.C., Department of Energy, Office of Biological and Environmental Research, 124 p.

Bailey, R.G., 1997, Map: Ecoregions of North America (rev.): Washington, D.C., U.S. Department of Agriculture, Forest Service, scale 1:15,000,000.

Bailey, J.W., and Thompson, F.R., III, 2007, Multiscale nest-site selection by black-capped vireos: The Journal of Wildlife Management, v. 71, p. 828–836.

Bale, A.M., 2009, Fire effects and litter accumulation dynamics in a montane longleaf pine ecosystem: Columbia, University of Missouri-Columbia, master's thesis, 103 p.

Bartlein, P.J., Hostetler, S.W., Shafer, S.L., Holman, J.O., and Solomon, A.M., 2008, Temporal and spatial structure in a daily wildfire-start dataset from the western United States (1986–96): International Journal of Wildland Fire, v. 17, p. 8–17.

Beatley, J.C., 1969, Biomass of desert winter annual plant populations in southern Nevada: Oikos, v. 20, p. 261–273.

Berry, K.H., Bailey, T.Y., and Anderson, K.M., 2006, Attributes of desert tortoise populations at the National Training Center, Central Mojave Desert, California, USA: Journal of Arid Environments, v. 67, p. 165–191.

Brandt, C.A., Rickard, W.H., and Cadoret, N.A., 1997, Vegetation studies: National Training Center, Fort Irwin, California: Pacific Northwest National Laboratory PNNL-11697, 45 p.

Brisbin, I.L., Jr., Standora, E.A., and Vargo, M.J., 1982, Body temperatures and behavior of American alligators during cold winter weather: The American Midland Naturalist, v. 107, p. 209–218.

Brooks, B.B., and Dean, T., 2008, Measuring the biological status of the U.S. breeding population of wood storks: Waterbirds, v. 31, Special Publication 1, p. 50–59.

Brooks, M.L., and Esque, T.C., 2002, Alien plants and fire in desert tortoise (Gopherus agassizii) habitat of the Mojave and Colorado Deserts: Chelonian Conservation and Biology, v. 4, p. 330–340.

Brooks, M.L., and Matchett, J.R., 2006, Spatial and temporal patterns of wildfires in the Mojave Desert, 1980–2004: Journal of Arid Environments, v. 67, p. 148–164.

Bryan, A.L., Jr., and Robinette, J.R., 2008, Breeding success of wood storks nesting in Georgia and South Carolina: Waterbirds, v. 31, Special Publication 1, p. 19–24.

Burns, R.M., and Honkala, B.H. (Technical Coordinators), 1990, Silvics of North America: 2. Hardwoods: Washington, D.C., U.S. Department of Agriculture, Forest Service, Agriculture Handbook 654, 877 p.

Butler, M.J., and Tappe, P.A., 2008, Relationships of red-cockaded woodpecker reproduction and foraging habitat characteristics in Arkansas and Louisiana: European Journal Wildlife Research, v. 54, p. 601–608.

Case, F.W., Jr., and Case, R.B., 1997, Trilliums: Portland, Oregon, Timber Press, Inc., 285 p.

Chabreck, R.H., 1973, Temperature variation in nests of the American alligator: Herpetologica, v. 29, p. 48–51.

Christensen, N.L., 2000, Vegetation of the southeastern coastal plain, Chapter 11 in Barbour, M.G., and Billings, W.D., eds., North American Terrestrial Vegetation, 2nd edition, Cambridge, UK, Cambridge University Press, p. 397–448.

Cleveland, W.S., 1993, Visualizing data: Summit, New Jersey, Hobart Press, 360 p.

Collins, W.D., Bitz, C.M., Blackmon, M.L., Bonan, G.B., Bretherton, C.S., Carton, J.A., Chang, P., Doney, S.C., Hack, J.J., Henderson, T.B., Kiehl, J.T., Large, W.G., McKenna, D.S., Santer, B.D., and Smith, R.D., 2006a, The Community Climate System Model Version 3 (CCSM3): Journal of Climate, v. 19, p. 2122–2143.

Collins, B., Sharitz, R., Madden, K., and Dilustro, J., 2006b, Comparison of sandhills and mixed pine-hardwood communities at Fort Benning, Georgia: Southeastern Naturalist, v. 5, p. 93–102.

Collins, B., Minchin, P.R., Dilustro, J., and Duncan, L., 2006c, Land use effects on groundlayer composition and regeneration of mixed pine hardwood forests in the Fall Line Sandhills, S.E. USA: Forest Ecology and Management, v. 226, p. 181–188.

Cook, E.R., Woodhouse, C.A., Eakin, C.M., Meko, D.M., and Stahle, D.W., 2004, Long-term aridity changes in the western United States: Science, v. 306, p. 1015–1018.

Coulter, M.C., and Bryan, A.L., Jr., 1995, Factors affecting reproductive success of wood storks (*Mycteria americana*) in east-central Georgia: The Auk, v. 112, p. 237–243.

Cramer, W., and Prentice, I.C., 1988, Simulation of regional soil moisture deficits on a European scale: Norsk Geografisk Tidsskrift, v. 42, p. 149–151.

Dai, A., 2006, Precipitation characteristics in eighteen coupled climate models: Journal of Climate, v. 19, p. 4605–4630.

Dale, V.H., Beyeler, S.C., and Jackson, B., 2002, Understory vegetation indicators of anthropogenic disturbance in longleaf pine forests at Fort Benning, Georgia, USA: Ecological Indicators, v. 1, p. 155–170.

Daly, C., 2006, Guidelines for assessing the suitability of spatial climate datasets: International Journal of Climatology, v. 26, p. 707–721.

Daly, C., Halbleib, M., Smith, J.I., Gibson, W.P., Doggett, M.K., Taylor, G.H., Curtis, J., and Pasteris, P.P., 2008, Physiographically sensitive mapping of climatological temperature and precipitation across the conterminous United States: International Journal of Climatology, v. 28, p. 2031–2064.

Dearborn, D.C., and Sanchez, L.L., 2001, Do golden-cheeked warblers select nest locations on the basis of patch vegetation?: The Auk, v. 118, p. 1052–1057.

Del Tredici, P., 2001, Sprouting in temperate trees: A morphological and ecological review: The Botanical Review, v. 67, p. 121–140.

Diemer, J.E., 1986, The ecology and management of the gopher tortoise in the southeastern United States: Herpetologica, v. 42, p. 125–133.

Dilustro, J., Collins, B., and Duncan, L., 2006, Land use history effects in mixed pine – hardwood forests at Fort Benning: Journal of the Torrey Botanical Society, v. 133, p. 460–467.

Dilustro, J.J., Collins, B.S., Duncan, L.K., and Sharitz, R.R., 2002, Soil texture, land-use intensity, and vegetation of Fort Benning upland forest sites: Journal of the Torrey Botanical Society, v. 129, p. 289–297.

Engstrom, R.T., and Evans, G.W., 1990, Hurricane damage to red-cockaded woodpecker (*Picoides borealis*) cavity trees: The Auk, v. 107, p. 608–610.

Esque, T.C., Schwalbe, C.R., DeFalco, L.A., Duncan, R.B., and Hughes, T.J., 2003, Effects of desert wildfires on desert tortoise (*Gopherus agassizii*) and other small vertebrates: The Southwestern Naturalist, v. 48, p. 103–111.

Fowler, N.L., and Dunlap, D.W., 1986, Grassland vegetation of the eastern Edwards Plateau: American Midland Naturalist, v. 115, p. 146–155.

Gan, J., 2004, Risk and damage of southern pine beetle outbreaks under global climate change: Forest Ecology and Management, v. 191, p. 61–71.

Gesch, D.B., 2007, The national elevation dataset, *in* Maune, D., ed., Digital elevation model technologies and applications: The DEM Users Manual, 2nd Edition: Bethesda, Maryland, American Society for Photogrammetry and Remote Sensing, p. 99–118.

Gesch, D., Oimoen, M., Greenlee, S., Nelson, C., Steuck, M., and Tyler, D., 2002, The national elevation dataset: Photogrammetric Engineering and Remote Sensing, v. 68, no. 1, p. 5–11.

Gilliam, F.S., and Platt, W.J., 1999, Effects of long-term fire exclusion on tree species composition and stand structure in an old-growth *Pinus palustris* (Longleaf pine) forest: Plant Ecology, v. 140, p. 15–26.

Giorgi, F., 2005, Climate change prediction: Climatic Change, v. 73, p. 239–265.

Giorgi, F., and Diffenbaugh, N., 2008, Developing regional climate change scenarios for use in assessment of effects on human health and disease: Climate Research, v. 36, p. 141–151.

Gonzales, E., and Hamrick, J.L., 2005, Distribution of genetic diversity among disjunct populations of the rare forest understory herb, *Trillium reliquum*: Heredity, doi:10.1038/sj.hdy.6800719.

Grzybowski, J.A., Tazik, D.J., and Schnell, G.D., 1994, Regional analysis of black-capped vireo breeding habitats: The Condor, v. 96, p. 512–544.

Guretzky, J.A., Anderson, A.B., and Fehmi, J.S., 2006, Grazing and military vehicle effects on grassland soils and vegetation: Great Plains Research, v. 16, p. 51–61.

Guyer, C., Birkhead, R., and Balbach, H., 2006, Effects of tracked-vehicle training activity on gopher tortoise (*Gopherus polyphemus*) behavior at Fort Benning, GA: U.S. Army Corps of Engineers ERDC/CERL TR–06–10, 17 p.

Hay, L.E., Wilby, R.L., and Leavesley, G.H., 2000, A comparison of delta change and downscaled GCM scenarios for three mountainous basins in the United States: Journal of the American Water Resources Association, v. 36, p. 387–397.

Hayden, T.J., Cornelius, J.D., Weinberg, H.J., Jette, L.L., and Melton, R.H., 2001, Endangered species management plan for Fort Hood, Texas; FY01–05: U.S. Army Corps of Engineers ERDC/CERL TR–01–26, 165 p.

Hazard, L.C., Shemanski, D.R., and Nagy, K.A., 2009, Nutritional quality of natural foods of juvenile desert tortoises (*Gopherus agassizii*): Energy, nitrogen, and fiber digestibility: Journal of Herpetology, v. 43, p. 38–48.

Heckel, C.D., and Leege, L.M., 2007, Life history and reproductive biology of the endangered *Trillium reliquum*: Plant Ecology, v. 189, p. 49–57.

Henen, B.T., Peterson, C.C., Wallis, I.R., Berry, K.H., and Nagy, K.A., 1998, Effects of climatic variation on field metabolism and water relations of desert tortoises: Oecologia, v. 117, p. 365–373.

Hereford, R., Webb, R.H., and Longpré, C.I., 2006, Precipitation history and ecosystem response to multidecadal precipitation variability in the Mojave Desert region, 1893–2001: Journal of Arid Environments, v. 67, p. 13–34.

Heyward, F., 1939, The relation of fire to stand composition of longleaf pine forests: Ecology, v. 20, p. 287–304.

Hickler, T., Smith, B., Sykes, M.T., Davis, M.B., Sugita, S., and Walker, K., 2004, Using a generalized vegetation model to simulate vegetation dynamics in the western Great Lakes region, USA, under alternative disturbance regimes: Ecology, v. 85, p. 519–530.

Hickler, T., Smith, B., Prentice, I.C., Mjofors, K., Miller, P., Arneth, A., and Sykes, M.T., 2008, CO_2 fertilization in temperate FACE experiments not representative of boreal and tropical forests: Global Change Biology, v. 14, p. 1–12.

Holder, C.D., 2000, Geography of *Pinus elliottii* Engelm. and *Pinus palustris* Mill. leaf life-spans in the southeastern U.S.A.: Journal of Biogeography, v. 27, p. 311–318.

Hunt, R.H., and Ogden, J.J., 1991, Selected aspects of nesting ecology of American alligators in the Okefenokee Swamp: Journal of Herpetology, v. 25, p. 448–453.

Johnson, F.L., 1982, Effects of tank training activities on botanical features at Fort Hood, Texas: The Southwestern Naturalist, v. 27, p. 309–314.

Karl, T.R., Melillo, J.M., and Peterson, T.C., eds., 2009, Global climate change impacts in the United States: Cambridge University Press, 188 p.

Kirkman, L.K., Drew, M.B., West, L.T., and Blood, E.R., 1998, Ecotone characterization between upland longleaf pine/wiregrass stands and seasonally-ponded isolated wetlands: Wetlands, v. 18, p. 346–364.

Kirkman, L.K., Mitchell, R.J., Helton, R.C., and Drew, M.B., 2001, Productivity and species richness across an environmental gradient in a fire-dependent ecosystem: American Journal of Botany, v. 88, p. 2119–2128.

Koca, D., Smith, B., and Sykes, M.T., 2006, Modelling regional climate change effects on Swedish ecosystems: Climatic Change, v. 78, p. 381–406.

Kroll, J.C., 1980, Habitat requirements of the Golden-cheeked warbler: Management implications: Journal of Range Management, v. 33, p. 60–65.

Krzysik, A.J., 1994, The desert tortoise at Fort Irwin, California: USACERL Technical Report EN-94/10, 99 p.

Küchler, A.W., 1993, Potential natural vegetation of the conterminous United States. Global ecosystems database version 2.0. Digital vector data in an Albers equal area conic polygon network and derived raster data on a 5 km by 5 km Albers equal area 590 · 940 grid, one independent and one dependent single-attribute spatial layer, 3,580,905 bytes in 13 files: Boulder, Colorado, National Oceanic and Atmospheric Administration, National Geophysical Data Center.

Lance, V.A., 2003, Alligator physiology and life history: the importance of temperature: Experimental Gerontology, v. 38, p. 801–805.

Landers, J.L., Van Lear, D.H., and Boyer, W.D., 1995, The longleaf pine forests of the southeast: Requiem or renaissance?: Journal of Forestry, v. 93, p. 39–44.

Lenihan, J.M., Bachelet, D., Neilson, R.P., and Drapek, R., 2008, Simulated response of conterminous United States ecosystems to climate change at different levels of fire suppression, CO_2 emission rate, and growth response to CO_2: Global and Planetary Change, v. 64, p. 16–25.

Maloney, K.O., Garten, C.T., Jr., and Ashwood, T.L., 2008, Changes in soil properties following 55 years of secondary forest succession at Fort Benning, Georgia, U.S.A.: Restoration Ecology, v. 16, p. 503–510.

Maraun, D., Wetterhall, F., Ireson, A.M., Chandler, R.E., Kendon, E.J., Widmann, M., Brienen, S., Rust, H.W., Sauter, T., Themel, M., Venema, V.K.C., Chun, K.P., Goodess, C.M., Jones, R.G., Onof, C., Vrac, M., and Thiele-Eich, I., 2010, Precipitation downscaling under climate change: Recent developments to bridge the gap between dynamical models and the end user: Reviews of Geophysics, v. 48, RG3003, doi:10.1029/2009RG000314.

Martin, K.L., and Kirkman, L.K., 2009, Management of ecological thresholds to re-establish disturbance-maintained herbaceous wetlands of the south-eastern USA: Journal of Applied Ecology, v. 46, p. 906–914.

McLemore, C., Kroh, G.C., and Pinder, J.E., III, 2004, *Juniperus ashei* (Cupressaceae): Physiognomy and age structure in three mature Texas stands: Sida, v. 21, p. 1107–1120.

McRae, W.A., Landers, J.L., and Garner, J.A., 1981, Movement patterns and home range of the gopher tortoise: American Midland Naturalist, v. 106, p. 165–179.

Medica, P.A., Bury, R.B., and Luckenbach, R.A., 1980, Drinking and construction of water catchments by the desert tortoise, *Gopherus agassizii*, in the Mojave Desert: Herpetologica, v. 36, p. 301–304.

Meehl, G.A., Covey, C., Delworth, T., Latif, M., McAvaney, B., Mitchell, J.F.B., Stouffer, R.J., and Taylor, K.E., 2007a, The WCRP CMIP3 multi-model dataset: A new era in climate change research: Bulletin of the American Meteorological Society, v. 88, p. 1383–1394.

Meehl, G.A., Stocker, T.F., Collins, W.D., Friedlingstein, P., Gaye, A.T., Gregory, J.M., Kitoh, A., Knutti, R., Murphy, J.M., Noda, A., Raper, S.C.B., Watterson, I.G., Weaver, A.J., and Zhao, Z.-C., 2007b, Global climate projections, *in* Solomon, S., Qin, D., Manning, M., Chen, Z., Marquis, M., Averyt, K.B., Tignor, M., and Miller, H.L., eds., Climate change 2007: The physical science basis, Contribution of Working Group I to the Fourth Assessment Report of the Intergovernmental Panel on Climate Change: Cambridge, United Kingdom and New York, N.Y., USA, Cambridge University Press, p. 747–845.

Miller, D.A., and White, R.A., 1998, A conterminous United States multilayer soil characteristics dataset for regional climate and hydrology modeling: Earth Interactions, v. 2, no. 2, p. 1–26.

Mitchell, T.D., and Jones, P.D., 2005, An improved method of constructing a database of monthly climate observations and associated high-resolution grids: International Journal of Climatology, v. 25, p. 693–712.

Mitchell, R.J., Hiers, J.K., O'Brien, J.J., Jack, S.B., and Engstrom, R.T., 2006, Silviculture that sustains: the nexus between silviculture, frequent prescribed fire, and conservation of biodiversity in longleaf pine forests of the southeastern United States: Canadian Journal of Forest Research, v. 36, p. 2724–2736.

Mote, P.W., and Salathé, E.P., Jr., 2010, Future climate in the Pacific Northwest: Climatic Change, v. 102, p. 29–50.

Mushinsky, H.R., and McCoy, E.D., 1994, Comparison of gopher tortoise populations on islands and on the mainland in Florida, *in* Bury, R.B., and Germano, D.J., eds., Biology of North American Tortoises: Fish and Wildlife Research, v. 13, p. 39–48.

Nakicenovic, N., Alcamo, J., Davis, G., de Vries, B., Fenhann, J., Gaffin, S., Gregory, K., Grübler, A., Jung, T.Y., Kram, T., Lebre La Rovere, E., Michaelis, L., Mori, S., Morita, T., Pepper, W., Pitcher, H., Price, L., Riahi, K., Roehrl, A., Rogner, H.-H., Sankovski, A., Schlesinger, M., Shukla, P., Smith, S., Swart, R., van Rooijen, S., Victor, N., and Dadi, Z., 2000, Special report on emissions scenarios, A special report of Working Group III of the Intergovernmental Panel on Climate Change: Cambridge, United Kingdom, Cambridge University Press, 599 p.

New, M., Hulme, M., and Jones, P., 1999, Representing twentieth-century space-time climate variability. Part I: Development of a 1961–90 mean monthly terrestrial climatology: Journal of Climate, v. 12, p. 829–856.

New, M., Hulme, M., and Jones, P., 2000, Representing twentieth-century space-time climate variability, part II: Development of 1901–96 monthly grids of terrestrial surface climate: Journal of Climate, v. 13, p. 2217–2238.

New, M., Lister, D., Hulme, M., and Makin, I., 2002, A high-resolution data set of surface climate over global land areas: Climate Research, v. 21, p. 1–25.

Olsen, L.M., Dale, V.H., and Foster, T., 2007, Landscape patterns as indicators of ecological change at Fort Benning, Georgia, USA: Landscape and Urban Planning, v. 79, p. 137–149.

Parmesan, C., 2006, Ecological and evolutionary responses to recent climate change: Annual Review of Ecology, Evolution, and Systematics, v. 37, p. 637–669.

Parry, M.L., Canziani, O.F., Palutikof, J.P., van der Linden, P.J., and Hanson, C.E., eds, 2007, Climate change 2007: Impacts, adaptation and vulnerability, Contribution of Working Group II to the Fourth Assessment Report of the Intergovernmental Panel on Climate Change: Cambridge, United Kingdom, Cambridge University Press, 976 p.

Patrick, T.S., Allison, J.R., and Krakow, G.A., 1995, Protected plants of Georgia: Social Circle, Georgia, Georgia Department of Natural Resources, 246 p.

Pederson, N., Varner, J.M., III, and Palik, B.J., 2008, Canopy disturbance and tree recruitment over two centuries in a managed longleaf pine landscape: Forest Ecology and Management, v. 254, p. 85–95.

Peterson, C.C., 1996, Anhomeostasis: Seasonal water and solute relations in two populations of the desert tortoise (*Gopherus agassizii*) during chronic drought: Physiological Zoology, v. 69, p. 1324–1358.

Pope, V., Gallani, M.L., Rowntree, P.R., and Stratton, R.A., 2000, The impact of new physical parameterizations in the Hadley Centre climate model: HadAM3: Climate Dynamics, v. 16, p. 123–146.

Prasad, A.M., Iverson, L.R., Matthews, S., and Peters, M., 2007-ongoing, A climate change atlas for 134 forest tree species of the Eastern United States (database): Delaware, Ohio, Northern Research Station, U.S. Department of Agriculture, Forest Service, available at: http://www.nrs.fs fed.us/atlas/tree.

Prentice, I.C., Cramer, W., Harrison, S.P., Leemans, R., Monserud, R.A., and Solomon, A.M., 1992, A global biome model based on plant physiology and dominance, soil properties and climate: Journal of Biogeography, v. 19, p. 117–134.

Prentice, I.C., Farquhar, G.D., Fasham, M.J.R., Goulden, M.L., Heimann, M., Jaramillo, V.J., Kheshgi, H.S., Le Quéré, C., Scholes, R.J., and Wallace, D.W.R., 2001, The carbon cycle and atmospheric carbon dioxide, *in* Houghton, J.T., Ding, Y., Griggs, D.J., Noguer, M., van der Linden, P.J., Dai, X., Maskell, K., and Johnson, C.A., eds., Climate change 2001: The scientific basis. Contribution of Working Group I to the Third Assessment Report of the Intergovernmental Panel on Climate Change: Cambridge, United Kingdom and New York, N.Y., USA, Cambridge University Press, 881 p.

Randall, D.A., Wood, R.A., Bony, S., Colman, R., Fichefet, T., Fyfe, J., Kattsov, V., Pitman, A., Shukla, J., Srinivasan, J., Stouffer, R.J., Sumi, A., and Taylor, K.E., 2007, Climate models and their evaluation, *in* Solomon, S., Qin, D., Manning, M., Chen, Z., Marquis, M., Averyt, K.B., Tignor, M., and Miller, H.L., eds., Climate change 2007: The physical science basis. Contribution of Working Group I to the Fourth Assessment Report of the Intergovernmental Panel on Climate Change: Cambridge, United Kingdom and New York, N.Y., USA, Cambridge University Press, p. 589–662.

Reemts, C.M., and Hansen., L.L., 2007, Slow recolonization of burned oak-juniper woodlands by Ashe juniper (*Juniperus ashei*): Ten years of succession after crown fire: Forest Ecology and Management, v. 255, p. 1057–1066.

Reidy, J.L., Thompson, F.R., III, and Peak, R.G., 2009, Factors affecting golden-cheeked warbler nest survival in urban and rural landscapes: Journal of Wildlife Management, v. 73, p. 407–413.

Richter, B.D., Mathews, R., Harrison, D.L., and Wigington, R., 2003, Ecologically sustainable water management: Managing river flows for ecological integrity: Ecological Applications, v. 13, p. 206–224.

Richter, S.C., Young, J.E., Seigel, R.A., and Johnson, G.N., 2001, Postbreeding movements of the dark gopher frog, *Rana sevosa* Goin and Netting: Implications for conservation and management: Journal of Herpetology, v. 35, p. 316–321.

Rudolph, D.C., and Conner, R.N., 1991, Cavity tree selection by red-cockaded woodpeckers in relation to tree age: Wilson Bulletin, v. 103, p. 458–467.

Rundel, P.W., Prigge, B., and Sharifi, M.R., 2007, The effect of amount and frequency of precipitation on seedling establishment and survival of Lane Mountain milkvetch (*Astragalus jaegerianus* Munz). Final project report for the Environmental Sciences Division of the Army Research Office for proposal number 48641-EV: University of California, Los Angeles, 71 p.

Sala, O.E., Chapin, F.S., III, Armesto, J.J., Berlow, E., Bloomfield, J., Dirzo, R., Huber-Sanwald, E., Huenneke, L.F., Jackson, R.B., Kinzig, A., Leemans, R., Lodge, D.M., Mooney, H.A., Oesterheld, M., Poff, N.L., Sykes, M.T., Walker, B.H., Walker, M., and Wall, D.H., 2000, Global biodiversity scenarios for the year 2100: Science, v. 287, p. 1770–1774.

Schnurr, J.L., and Collins, B.S., 2007, Influences on oak and pine establishment with time since fire in sandhills *Pinus palustris* (longleaf pine) forests: Southeastern Naturalist, v. 6, p. 523–534.

Scinocca, J.F., McFarlane, N.A., Lazare, M., Li, J., and Plummer, D., 2008, The CCCma third generation AGCM and its extension into the middle atmosphere: Atmospheric Chemistry and Physics, v. 8, p. 7055–7074.

Sitch S., Smith, B., Prentice, I.C., Arneth, A., Bondeau, A., Cramer, W., Kaplan, J.O., Levis, S., Lucht, W., Sykes, M.T., Thonicke, K., and Venevsky, S., 2003, Evaluation of ecosystem dynamics, plant geography and terrestrial carbon cycling in the LPJ dynamic global vegetation model: Global Change Biology, v. 9, p. 161–185.

Smith, B., Prentice, I.C., and Sykes, M.T., 2001, Representation of vegetation dynamics in the modelling of terrestrial ecosystems: comparing two contrasting approaches within European climate space: Global Ecology & Biogeography, v. 10, p. 621–637.

Solomon, A.M., 1986, Transient response of forests to CO_2-induced climate change: simulation modeling experiments in eastern North America: Oecologia, v. 68, p. 567–579.

Spalding, M.G., Folk, M.J., Nesbitt, S.A., Folk, M.L., and Kiltie, R., 2009, Environmental correlates of reproductive success for introduced resident whooping cranes in Florida: Waterbirds, v. 32, p. 538–547.

Tazik, D.J., Cornelius, J.D., and Abrahamson, C.A., 1993a, Status of the black-capped vireo at Fort Hood, Texas, volume I: Distribution and abundance: USACERL Technical Report EN-94/01, v. I, 54 p.

Tazik, D.J., Grzybowski, J.A., and Cornelius, J.D., 1993b, Status of the black-capped vireo at Fort Hood, Texas, volume II: Habitat: USACERL Technical Report EN-94/01, v. II, 41 p.

Thompson, R.S., Anderson, K.H., and Bartlein, P.J., 1999, Atlas of relations between climatic parameters and distributions of important trees and shrubs in North America—Introduction and conifers: U.S. Geological Survey Professional Paper 1650–A, 269 p.

U.S. Fish and Wildlife Service, 1984, Endangered and threatened wildlife and plants, U.S. breeding population of the wood stork determined to be endangered: Federal Register, v. 9, p. 7332–7335.

U.S. Fish and Wildlife Service, 1987, Endangered and threatened wildlife and plants; reclassification of the American alligator to threatened due to similarity of appearance throughout the remainder of its range: Federal Register, v. 52, p. 21059–21064.

U.S. Fish and Wildlife Service, 1988, Endangered and threatened wildlife and plants, determination of endangered status for the relict trillium: Federal Register, v. 53, p. 10879–10884.

U.S. Fish and Wildlife Service, 1990a, Endangered and threatened wildlife and plants, final rule to list the golden-cheeked warbler as endangered: Federal Register, v. 55, p. 53153–53160.

U.S. Fish and Wildlife Service, 1990b, Endangered and threatened wildlife and plants, determination of threatened status for the Mojave population of the desert tortoise: Federal Register, v. 55, no. 63, p. 12178–12191.

U.S. Fish and Wildlife Service, 2003, Recovery plan for the red-cockaded woodpecker (*Picoides borealis*): second revision: Atlanta, Georgia, U.S. Fish and Wildlife Service, 296 p.

U.S. Fish and Wildlife Service, 2008, Lane Mountain milk-vetch (*Astragalus jaegerianus*), 5-year review: Summary and evaluation: Ventura, California, U.S. Fish and Wildlife Service, 20 p.

Van Lear, D.H., Carroll, W.D., Kapeluck, P.R., and Johnson, R., 2005, History and restoration of the longleaf pine-grassland ecosystem: Implications for species at risk: Forest Ecology and Management, v. 211, p. 150–165.

Varner, J.M., III, Gordon, D.R., Putz, F.E., and Hiers, J.K., 2005, Restoring fire to long-unburned *Pinus palustris* ecosystems: Novel fire effects and consequences for long-unburned ecosystems: Restoration Ecology, v. 13, p. 536–544.

Varner, J.M., III, Hiers, J.K., Ottmar, R.D., Gordon, D.R., Putz, F.E., and Wade, D.D., 2007, Overstory tree mortality resulting from reintroducing fire to long-unburned longleaf pine forests: the importance of duff moisture: Canadian Journal of Forest Research, v. 37, p. 1349–1358.

Varner, J.M., III, and Kush, J.S., 2004, Remnant old-growth longleaf pine (*Pinus palustris* Mill.) savannas and forests of the southeastern USA: Status and threats: Natural Areas Journal, v. 24, p. 141–149.

Walther, G.-R., Post, E., Convey, P., Menzel, A., Parmesan, C., Beebee, T.J.C., Fromentin, J.-M., Hoegh-Guldberg, O., and Bairlein, F., 2002, Ecological responses to recent climate change: Nature, v. 416, p. 389–395.

Wiens, J.A., and Bachelet, D., 2010, Matching the multiple scales of conservation with the multiple scales of climate change: Conservation Biology, v. 24, p. 51–62.

Wilson, D.S., Mushinsky, H.R., and McCoy, E.D., 1994, Home range, activity, and use of burrows of juvenile gopher tortoises in central Florida *in* Bury, R.B., and Germano, D.J., eds., Biology of North American Tortoises: Fish and Wildlife Research, v. 13, p. 147–160.

Wink, R.L., and Wright, D.J., 1973, Effects of fire on an Ashe juniper community: Journal of Range Management, v. 26, p. 326–329.

Wramneby, A., Smith, B., Zaehle, S., and Sykes, M.T., 2008, Parameter uncertainties in the modelling of vegetation dynamics—Effects on tree community structure and ecosystem functioning in European forest biomes: Ecological Modelling, v. 216, p. 277–290.

Zaehle, S., Sitch, S., Smith, B., and Hatterman, F., 2005, Effects of parameter uncertainties on the modeling of terrestrial biosphere dynamics: Global Biogeochemical Cycles, v. 19, GB3020, doi:10.1029/2004GB002395.